THE DILEMMA OF BEING CHOSEN

M.C. VAN RENSBURG

authorHOUSE®

AuthorHouse™ UK
1663 Liberty Drive
Bloomington, IN 47403 USA
www.authorhouse.co.uk
Phone: 0800.197.4150

Published by AuthorHouse 08/16/2016

ISBN: 978-1-5049-8840-7 (sc)
ISBN: 978-1-5049-8841-4 (e)

To my wife and son, who have been a source of indescribable support and indubitable inspiration in often unimaginably difficult circumstances.

PREFACE

Believing in God necessitates believing in design. I firmly believe that not a single person on the earth is here without a God-ordained purpose. In fact, it would be illogical to argue that we have appeared on earth randomly. Our lives on earth is in a very narrow sense a walk through time. But, as we walk through time, we normally reach a point where we feel and sense that there has to be more to life than the day-to-day monotony we may sometimes experience. Often this monotony is disrupted when we experience an abrupt change of scenery in our lives brought about by various situations and circumstances. We are not necessarily always ready for such disruptions. Almost being forced to make the necessary transitions, as it will never get done under normal conditions, we feel caught in the trenches between what we are used to and what we should give ourselves to. This book is about that place where we understand and sense that we have a purpose, a calling to do something specific, but where we also realise that our purpose will not crystallise as easily as we may have thought. When we have the sense of purpose in our hearts, it means that God has selected us, has chosen us, for such. Being chosen by God, for whatever task, in itself is a tremendous honour, but with such an honour comes the dilemma that the vessel of choice has to face in relation to that specific calling. As vessels of choice, we are seldom naturally aligned to what has been placed in our hearts. Long after God has made His choice in choosing the vessel, the vessel more often than not struggles with the context of his or her life in relation to being chosen. It can become an incredible battle to align oneself to that which has been birthed in one's heart. When we come into contact with the fact that God has chosen us for a particular role, purpose is born in our heart. From the inception of such purpose to its manifestation, we are in need of divine favour to bridge that gap. Understanding the triangular relationship between being chosen, having purpose, and being favoured is key to making a successful transition from where one is to where one has to end up. The story of Mary, Joseph, and the birth of Jesus aptly provides the necessary background for the discussion of these themes.

Throughout the pages of this book, I try not to offer conventional views on the subject of being chosen, being favoured and having purpose.

The introduction of this book, as is the case with the start of each chapter (with the exception of the Conclusion), is purely fictional and is loosely based on the facts and events surrounding the lives of Mary and Joseph at the time of their having been chosen to be the earthly parents of Jesus. I think that this fictionalisation makes for interesting, easy, and relaxed reading, but it also leaves a reader with powerful visuals. I trust that you will enjoy reading this book, and I pray that the Lord will bless, promote, and favour you greatly in what He has planned and purposed for your life.

Warmly,

M. C. Van Rensburg

ACKNOWLEDGEMENTS

To my parents, family and friends for their unwavering
support. Your encouragement and invaluable
contributions gave substance to this book.

Towards the later part of writing this book, I lost one
of my dearest friends, Willem Samuel Swartbooi, who
had been a great inspiration as a friend, comrade,
and brother throughout the time we shared.

Thank you.

TABLE OF CONTENTS

INTRODUCTION

It was a summit discussing Their original intent and plan. Producing correction to the deviation was at the heart of the discussion. The invasion was high on the agenda, in particular the logistics thereof. In front of Them was a layout of Planet Earth, which enjoys premium status and an unambiguous bias in Their vested interest. As gold is often perceived as the darling of metals and the lion dubbed the king of the beasts of the wild, so is Earth's prominence amongst the planets. It is not the largest of the planets; that honour belongs to Jupiter. It is not the brightest; that glory befits Venus. It is not central to the solar system; that is the grandeur of the sun. But Earth's prominence to Them, is found in what it lodges: the crown of creation, humankind. Their undivided consideration for the well-being of humankind had elicited this confab. Decisions were made at speeds that made lightning look static. Yet those decisions were made with pinpoint accuracy and unimaginable meticulousness. Still, the marvellous speed, accuracy, and thoroughness did not compare to the astounding unison. The dialogue was without debate or contradiction. Instead, it was executed in seamless unanimity.

There is an enemy[1] out there, a ruthless eradicator, one seeking to destroy the soul of the crown of creation, humankind. The eternal well-being of the human race is at stake. Just as created matter cannot be hazardous to its creator, so does this enemy pose no threat to Them – but to flesh and blood he does. The adversary's methodology and thinking is mentioned only in relation to the potential threat he poses to the good of Their crown. Otherwise, this enemy is just a negligible entity.

Who fits the profile of caring for the Word in the fragility and dependency of a baby? Where will the Word be incarnated? These are two vital and strategic questions asked in relation to the invasion. A conclusion about the way the enemy thinks was reached through the following considerations: The foe discards that which appears insignificant. His pride and his lofty heart were the causes of his disfavour. His predisposition towards high and perceived glorious things has flawed his understanding of the concept of significance.

A gaping fragility was unlocked in the antagonist's demeanour, a weakness worth exposing. With these truths in mind, the place of Jesus's birth had to be decided upon. Apart from the place, the womb in which to hide Him had to be found. Their eyes searched the Earth like laser beams and stopped at a portion of land that was promised to the descendants of Abraham, a province called Galilee, and in particular a town called Nazareth. The search then probed through Nazareth, seeking a vessel, and stopped at Mary. Nazareth appeared to be a small enough town to hide His identity, whilst the womb of Mary seemed humble and mundane enough to conceal Him from the evil one.

The summit was concluded with a message to send for Gabriel. A blaze of joy and relief swept through the heavens as the rumour of Gabriel's being called reached the celestial crowd. The inhabitants of the heavens knew that Gabriel was *the* messenger of good news. A tangible vibe of excitement was felt by the inhabitants of paradise as they shared a silent confidence that the potential of the crown of creation would be restored. Gabriel, in the interim, rushed through the courts of heaven. He entered the meeting place and greeted Them, saying "Holy, Holy, Holy." Gabriel was immediately referred to a blueprint of Earth stretched out in front of Them. His attention was brought to Nazareth. A picture of Mary, engraved in Their heart, was shown to him.

The assignment was as follows: "Go and tell Mary she has been chosen as a vessel to harbour the eternal seed of the Word. Tell her that she has been highly favoured to conceive the Saviour of the world."

There was nothing spectacular about Mary. She was just a commoner with a typical small-town-girl mentality, a young girl who sometimes secretly wished to be in the shoes of those who were more famous and richer. At times, the prosaic nature of her life caused her subtle frustration, but of late she had felt a sense of fulfilment. A feeling of completion had entrapped her soul since her engagement to the carpenter, Joseph. Elizabeth, her cousin, and Joseph happened to be the two most treasured people in her life. It was regrettable that Elizabeth did not live any closer, as Mary would have loved to visit her more often. Regularly, Mary's thoughts were lost in contemplation of what a wonderful man she had found in Joseph. She appeared to be having the best of what human companionship could offer, but there was still a silent missing piece to it all. A piece to the puzzle she could not readily put her finger on. She had an indelible sense that there should be even more to life than what she currently had. And at that moment, whilst caught-up with the daily chores of life, Gabriel appeared to her, conveying the message from the summit. Mary's life would never be the same again. The monotony was forever broken. The silent missing piece, namely, purpose, had been found.

> Luke 1:28: "And having come in, the angel said to her, "Rejoice, highly favoured one, the Lord is with you."

The declaration that Mary was highly favoured and had been chosen by God for the special purpose of conceiving the Saviour of the world had an impact on every facet of Mary's understanding of God and of herself, as can be deduced from her encomium:

> It produced worship and praise in her.
> "My soul magnifies the Lord" (Luke 1:46).
>
> It challenged the perception and perspective she had about herself.
> "For He has regarded the lowly state of His maidservant" (Luke 1:48).
>
> It changed the driving force of her life.
> "Let it be to me according to Your Word" (Luke 1:38).
>
> It caused growth.
> "He has put down the might from their thrones and exalted the lowly" (Luke 1:52).

It challenged her thinking.
"He scattered the proud in the imagination of
their hearts" (Luke 1:48).

It produced prosperity.
"For behold henceforth all generations will call
me blessed" (Luke 1:48).

* * *

I believe that we would err by thinking that our lives can remain untouched from the impact and effect of our being chosen for whatever purpose. In the ensuing pages, we will discuss this and other facets pertaining to being chosen and favoured. I argue that an understanding of the triangular interworking of being favoured, being chosen, and having a purpose is indispensable if we are to successfully produce what has been placed in our hearts to produce. A lack of understanding in this regard would make vague to us what our own responsibility in the process is and what God's responsibility is. Our being chosen is God's prerogative, and so is our purpose. Favour, I believe, is the side to this triangle that is needed in order to bring fulfilment to our being chosen and to whatever purpose has been placed in our heart. But favour, although given by God, is the one facet of the triangle over which we have control- in the sense that we can determine either allowance or disallowance of the functioning of God's favour over our lives. Hence we witness the phenomenon of gifted and talented people (they are chosen and have a sense of purpose) who do not fulfil their potential because their hand is not on the favour lever. So I would start off by arguing for a more holistic approach to, and definition of, favour. Thereafter I will discuss the effect of being chosen, and certain facets of purpose to cement the triangular interworking.

CHAPTER 1

WHAT IS FAVOUR?

"My soul magnifies the Lord"

Luke 1:46

Grace is simply another word for God's tumbling, rumbling reservoir of strength and protection. It comes at us not occasionally or miserly but constantly and aggressively, wave upon wave.

Max Lucado

Mary is still trying to come to terms with the full meaning and impact of the divine encounter. At times it appears surreal, but then she reiterates to herself the reality of that life-altering experience. The words that the angel had uttered resound in her like a river flooding its bank. Sent into a stardust state, Mary cannot verbalise to anyone the depth and impact of that moment. No earthbound creature would believe her anyway. Daily, she ponders on the words "highly favoured" as she revisits the declaration in her mind. Mary is filled with such a sense of occasion, but there is also an underlying curious uncertainty flooding her soul. She is uncertain about the full meaning of what the angel conveyed to her, about where all this is leading. Days appear to be unfolding too slowly as her curiosity produces an earnest impatience. One moment, Mary thinks she understands everything, but in the next moment she finds herself completely confused by the awesomeness of the words that the angel had used to appraise her. Her mind is undividedly set on unravelling this divine riddle, which appears to be drawing her farther away from the daily activities in her little town. The predominant questions perplexing her mind are, "Why me?" and "What does it truly mean to be highly favoured by God?" As an ordinary, small-town young girl, Mary does not quite know what to expect now that God has made this declaration over her life. She also realises that there could be a vast discrepancy between what she wants "highly favoured" to mean and what it could turn out to truly mean. "What if being highly favoured does not fit my presupposed framework of favour?" she asks herself. "What if my expectations are misaligned?" she asks. "What if this entails more than what I am prepared for?" she ponders. The people closest to Mary have come to notice her preoccupation. She is not yet ready to disclose her thoughts to her inner circle. For now, she soldiers on in her quest of wanting to see and understand the extent of what it means to be favoured.

* * *

I am of the opinion that the question of what it means to be highly favoured is one worth asking. It is also one that is important to probe. In church circles today, talking or preaching about favour has almost become cliché. It has become part of the jargon. Our understanding (or the lack thereof) of what being favoured means is often informed by our circumstances. Often, situations, good or bad, hinge our framework, which leads us to attempt to force-fit our presupposed ideas into the concept of being favoured by God. I would suggest that to optimally appropriate being favoured, we should not even allow experience, good or bad, to inform our understanding. A discrepancy between what we want favour to mean and what the true meaning of favour is would inevitably lead to disappointment. Misaligned expectations always produce fruitless toil and, ultimately, the abortion of purpose. So how can we get to a meaningful definition of divine favour?

The *Collins Compact Dictionary*[1] defines favour as follows:

- An approving attitude
- An act done out of goodwill
- Bias at the expense of others

In addition to declaring Mary to be "highly favoured", the angel said the following at the birth of Jesus:

> "Glory to God in the highest, and on earth peace, goodwill toward men" (Luke 2:14).

In the definition of *The Collins Compact Dictionary* and the above scripture, we can see five vital components – glory to God, peace, an approving attitude, bias, and goodwill –emerging to help give us a better understanding of the meaning of being favoured. I think that it is fundamental to understand how these components fit with the concept of being favoured. The composition would look as follows:

Component	Result of	Producing
Glory to God	Relationship	A sense of purpose
Peace	Relationship	A correct view of the Creator
Approving attitude	Submission	An understanding that we matter
Bias	Purpose	Celebration and interconnectedness
Goodwill	Motive	Inner peace

Component 1: Glory to God

The act of glorifying God is an essential part of being favoured, as it produces a sense of higher purpose. Favour devoid of purpose amounts to bribery and lust.

The act of glorifying God is essentially an acknowledgement that we are neither the end nor the beginning of everything. It is from this base that we become receptive to a higher purpose. The people who lived during Paul's day are an apt illustration of what can happen if we deviate from the "simple" act of glorifying God. When reading about their gross indulgences, one cannot help but wonder how they got to such a position of profligacy. The answer to that question, though, is given in:

4

> Romans 1:21: "Because that, when they knew
> God: they glorified Him not as God, neither was
> thankful but become vain in their imaginations,
> and their foolish heart was darkened."

From this verse, we observe that glorifying God is not merely a choice; it also serves as a dividing line between light and darkness, determining which will enter and dominate our life. The act of glorifying God denotes humility whereas darkness of heart emanates when we deviate from that humility. In the words of Nebuchadnezzar when he repented of his pride, "I lifted mine eyes unto heaven and my understanding returned unto me" (Daniel 5:34), do we deduce that glorifying God keeps the heart humble and the mind sane. A call to a lifestyle of glorifying God is not a call to practise a religion or to perform sanctimonious acts; rather, it is an invitation for the Lord to walk us through the path of life. It constitutes a call to sanity and purpose. It is from such a walk and lifestyle that the equilateral triangle of worshipping God, serving people, and being content within oneself finds its equality. None of us can effectively live a lifestyle of glorifying God if one of those elements is disproportionate to the others. Ultimately, whatever we have been favoured with cannot function in a vacuum. It has to be received from God, and then the receiver has to act as a conduit to someone else. Hence, a genuine lifestyle of glorifying God shows how we relate to God, to ourselves, and to others, and is the bedrock and conduit for receiving divine favour and purpose.

Component 2: Peace (on earth)

Our relationship with our fellows, which essentially drives and determines the peace on earth, is an essential part of being favoured, as it attest to our view and understanding of our Creator.

Peace on earth[2] has always been God's desire. Inherently, peace conveys the ideas of harmony and balance. It is not difficult to perceive that there is no balance or harmony on the earth today. Earthquakes, tsunamis, wars, crimes, hatred, etc., are all testimonies to the imbalance in creation. Paul, the author of the book of Romans, wrote,[3] "The whole creation groans and travails in pain." From scientists to politicians to psychologists to preachers, many people are trying to explain from various angles this one phenomenon of the earth. All are endeavouring to come up with a solution to what the Bible describes as a "creation ... in pain". Pain implies a deviation from what is normal, a violation of intent and purpose. The presence of pain, whether physical or psychological, in creation at large or in a human life, always indicates abnormality, irrationality, and malfunctioning. Most, if not all, of the melancholic aberrations in creation can be seen to be a direct result of humankind's inhumanity to humankind. Earth, as the planet favoured to contain human life, is making its displeasure and pain known through what we have come to understand as (un)natural disasters.

Peace on earth concerns the horizontal axis of our relationships. The message from the Bible is simple: you do not have access to the invisible Lord unless you live right, make right, and do right to your visible neighbour. First John asks the question, "How can you love the Lord whom you have never seen and hate your brother whom you do see?" Our relationship with the invisible God is reflected in our relationship with visible humankind. How we esteem the next person is, more than any church service we may have attended or any scripture we may have studied, an accurate attestation of our understanding of our Creator. The mark of a favoured person, according to the example set by Jesus (Luke 2:52), is found in his or her having favour with *both* God and people.

Component 3: An approving attitude

Seeking the approval of God is an essential part of being favoured, not for His sake but for ours. It is also an indication of our understanding that we matter.

We find ourselves living in what is being referred to as the postmodern era, an epoch where the line between right and wrong has been blurred like never before.

We are indeed a generation of people who do
not quite understand that we matter.

We have invented new rules for almost everything. We have invented our own god, one with no opinion or feeling. This god takes no stance towards anything; is never pleased or displeased; and never likes or dislikes anything. In short, we have created a god who is indifferent to human behaviour.

But the very concept of divine favour implies that God has a preference. When one looks more closely at this indifferent mentality, one sees that we are indeed a generation of people who do not quite understand that we matter. We don't reasonably comprehend how we are cosmically interlinked.

This is clearly demonstrated when hardship befell Job, he reasoned with his friends that he had not done anything wrong. He then insisted that he wanted a hearing with God. His friends replied by asking him that even if he had sinned, how would his sin matter to God? Succinctly they were telling him, "You don't matter to such an extent." In the end, Job's friends were proven wrong, as Job did get his requested hearing with God. This clearly illustrates that we matter because we have been created by God. What befalls us matter to Him. Our lack of understanding that we do matter, in many respect, stem from the fact that we are not always conscious of the fact that we have been created and did not appear on earth randomly.

There are a lot of theories and philosophies about the inception and existence of humankind, but none of these hold truer to the human experience than does the Genesis narrative of creation. God in His sovereignty decided to create humankind when He said, "Let Us make man in our image and after our likeness."[4] Previous acts of creation displayed God's craftsmanship, but the creation of humankind required an even deeper level of giving from God. He had to give Himself and not just of Himself in order to have a being after His image and likeness. On the basis of that fact it becomes implausible that we do not matter.

Component 4: Bias

Understanding that God has a particular bias towards each and every person is an essential part of being favoured, as it stirs us to celebrate our interconnectedness rather than to promote our fragmentation.

Inherently, favour means bias. Favouring someone or something implies that this happens at the expense of an alternative[5]. God's choosing earth as an abode for humankind means that our planet was chosen at the expense of other planets that might have served the same purpose. So earth was favoured. Humanity's being chosen to be made in God's image and likeness was done at the expense of animals that might have served the same purpose. So humankind was favoured. When the angel appeared unto Mary to pronounce her "highly favoured", she was pronounced so at the expense of others who might have served the same purpose. So, Mary was favoured.

As each one of us is unique in this world, so is the purpose to which God has called us. In other words, God has a particular bias towards each one of us in relation to what He has purposed for us. It is that particular bias that creates the predicate for divine favour. That special ability or gifting with which you have been blessed is the angle of God's bias upon you. Mary and her cousin Elizabeth were both pregnant with children who would serve distinct, yet interconnected, purposes. The two women did not envy each other based on the distinct purposes their children would end up serving. Instead, when Mary visited Elizabeth, the two of them celebrated the respective biasness they had received from the Lord. They understood both the bias and the interconnectedness in God's purpose: Jesus would need John, and John would need Jesus. An important lesson we should learn from Mary and Elizabeth is this: favoured people should connect with each other when their respective purposes are in the embryonic stage in order to celebrate their interconnectedness.

Component 5: Goodwill

Understanding God's goodwill is an essential part of being favoured, as we, at times, will experience a discrepancy between our circumstances and our mental understanding of being favoured.

Goodwill is a function of motive. As a concept, divine favour has its essence in the goodwill of God towards humankind. It speaks of the nature and motive of God towards humanity. Do I trust God's motive for my life? Can I trust God's motive for my life? The theoretical answer to these two questions is an obvious yes. The practical test, however, could prove to be difficult for most of us. The truth is that reconciling His goodwill motive with our painful experiences of the past or in the present could be a steep mountain for many us to climb. Part of the dilemma could be the sometimes fragmented view we have of events as they unfold in our lives. The second truth to consider is that not all of our experiences were instigated by God. We happen to be free moral agents capable of exercising the gift of choice. Reality, though, testifies that not all the choices we have made are healthy ones. God, however, has a different vantage point when He looks at us.

The goodwill of God is that aspect of His
nature that does not guarantee a smooth ride,
but rather ensures a safe landing.

He takes not an isolated view, but a holistic view, of the events unfolding in our lives. In adopting the same view, we would stumble upon two truths:

1. One or more bad evens do not define a person and therefore cannot be the catalyst for future events.

2. The goodwill of God is the aspect of His nature that does not guarantee a smooth ride, but rather ensure a safe landing. God's goodwill is that sovereign power which, when we give allowance to it, works the bad that has befallen us for our good. The psalmist David experienced this, as made clear by his statement, "Surely goodness and mercy shall follow me."

We can thus conclude that divine favour is:

God's approving attitude, goodwill, and bias towards any person through a living relationship with Him and through that person's healthy relationship with his or her fellows.

"My soul magnifies the Lord" (Luke 1:46).

CHAPTER 2

IF I AM FAVOURED, WHY IS MY WORLD FALLING APART?

For He has regarded the lowly state of His maidservant.

Luke 1:48

When you are floating in a sea of helplessness, you must find some concrete way to express your freely embraced deepest commitment.

John Ortberg

Why she has been chosen remains hidden to Mary. In her mind, she draws parallels between herself and various others, but she fails to see the difference between herself and others. In fact, when looking at the lives of those to whom she compares her own, she even sometimes struggles to view herself as an approximate. The mystery of God's bias towards her is sealed to her understanding. Week after week she had heard the prophetic readings from the synagogue about the coming of the Messiah. Readings from Isaiah, e.g. "Behold a virgin shall conceive, and bear a son, and shall call his name Emmanuel," she has heard numerous times. That she has been selected to bring fulfilment to a prophetic word spoken many years before she was born is a wonder Mary cannot wrestle into silence. It is a thought that instigates a tug-of-war between restraint and ecstasy. She finds herself wiggling at the fulcrum of these extremes. She cannot break free in blissful joy, as Joseph is still ignorant of the happenings of the summit in heaven. "How will I explain this to him?" she asks herself. "How will he believe me?" the thought anxiously registers, "How do I explain this to the religious leaders?" But these thoughts are secondary, swiftly giving way to the divine riddle: "Why was I chosen?" The secrecy of God's choice provokes Mary's curiosity as the thought corners her into interrogating her own worth. "If God chose me to be the mother of the Saviour of the world, then I should be worth more than what societal systems would want me to believe," she deduces.

The people of Palestine had seen and heard of many empires coming and going, from the Babylonian empire to the Persian empire to the Grecian empire, the last becoming the dominant political power under Alexander the Great. But now they find themselves living under what is arguably the greatest empire the world has ever seen: the Roman empire. Power has completely passed out of Jewish hands, and the religious sects – the Sadducees, the Pharisees, the Scribes, and the Zealots – lack the impetus to bring about change. The Sadducees have secularised religion. The Pharisees have made religion heartless by loading it with legalistic observances. The Scribes professionalised religion, whilst the Zealots made religion a political premise urging violence against Rome. As a catalyst for change, the religious atmosphere is impotent. Added to this the political tone is oppressive, leaving little room for ambition, freethinking, and self-expression. The oppressive air has filtered through to every facet of society and has ultimately funnelled to the individual. It has become apparent that religion and politics, the two most powerful platforms, have failed the ordinary person at the proletarian level. Attributable to the tyrannical political atmosphere, most of the people have a twisted and restrained perception of themselves and of their worth. Whereas fatuous legalism has rendered the religious order of the day feeble and far too frail to produce the needed paradigm shift, the fatal failure of both politics and religion has brought about an almost tangible expectancy for the Messiah amongst the people. Through the withered religious grapevine, the people have heard about a Messiah to come. In their restricted understanding, they believe that this Messiah will start a revolution against the domineering political system in the fashion of the Maccabean revolt led by Matthias and his five sons. This revolution would build a military power strong enough to overthrow the Roman grip.

Meanwhile, after having heard the celestial Word, Mary suspects that the desired change is going to come through neither politics nor religion. The words "You are highly favoured," from the angel of God, have brought to her an internal revolution. Inwardly, she finds herself a nonconformist to the religious and political tenets. She increasingly has the impression that God does not value people the way humanly devised systems do. Her perception of herself as being not worth much started being heavily challenged once she heard the Word. At times she does struggle to allow herself to enjoy her newfound freedom as she progressively breaks through the previous limitations of her "lowly estate" perceptions. Mary discerns a vast difference between the atmosphere of the world she lives in and the one she experienced when the angel brought her the good tidings. There is a gaping discrepancy between the two worlds. She happens to find herself in the balance.

* * *

Why, when we are being chosen, does it feel as if our world is falling apart? This is the question we have to probe and understand. In John 15:19, Jesus said to His disciples, "I have chosen you out of the world." which is a very profound message from Jesus to His disciples – and to every one of His followers today. The irony of being chosen is this: followers of Christ are chosen *out* of the world to live *in* the world. The place from where we are chosen and the one in which we live are two very different places. When we find ourselves in between these two worlds, a tug-of-war begins inside us. The truth is that although we are called out of the world, we, whilst living in the world, will find that the atmosphere and spirit of the world want to infiltrate us. It is this infiltration that sets us on a collision course with ourselves. On the one hand, we know we have been favoured for a particular task; on the other hand, we struggle with the infiltration from the world in which we live. Unless the atmosphere of our mind matches that of the world from which we are favoured, we will always experience patches of great friction. The reality is that we are seldom, if ever, naturally aligned to that which we are being called to do.

"Why does God not practise 'DIY' and omit humankind from the value chain of favour?" we may want to ask. I believe that when God decided to create a being "in His image and likeness", He opted for a collaboration between humanity and Divinity as an operating model, as far as the affairs of the earth are concerned. This is the very reason why we pray and ask that God's will be done "on earth as it is in heaven."[1] Hence, we have talent and a gifting as the prerogative of the Lord, but aligning ourselves to such grace is our responsibility as humans. Although at any stage of our lives we are ready for selection for a particular task, we are not necessarily fit for our purpose. At the time when the disciples were chosen, they were not necessarily fit for their purpose. We are no different. It is because of exactly this that we are in need of a change process, to bring about the necessary alignment. Although I want to believe that we can align without the change process, I remain unsure whether we can indeed change to the necessary degree without the concentration of the often autocratic force of the change process.

Although at any stage of our lives, we are ready
for selection for a particular task, we are not
necessarily fit for our purpose.

I think it is important that we establish a few generic realities, irrespective of circumstance, that present themselves whenever we go into and through a change process, the goal of which is to align us better to the world from which we have been chosen. The story of Jesus and His disciples (in Mark 4:35–39) having to cross from one site to another in stormy weather conveys at least eight such realities relating to the change process to ultimately align us.

Reality 1: Through the change process, we learn that being favoured does not imply being shielded or exempted from the often dark realities of life

---

Mark 4:35: "Evening was come."

Jesus chose for this transition to happen when the "evening was come". The timing of the transition itself brings about its own uncertainties. Whatever seeds of bias the Lord has placed on the inside of us can only sprout when the, "evening has come". It is when the evening clouds gather and then circle around our ambitions and sincere intentions that we start dying a secret death within. The future emerges as bleak and hopeless. Dreams, resolutions, and visions appear as slippery as an eel. Nobel plans become unstuck, slipping through our hands like grains of sand. Something appears wrong, but we can't figure it out and we have seemingly no control over it. Things don't hinge together when the evening has come. The "evening" disconnects us from the known and the predictable. At times we soldier on, with no point of reference to help us determine where, and how, everything will work out. As we progress through the low-hanging clouds of the evening, we find that layer after layer of our strength, resources, and plans is peeled away until we find ourselves naked with nothing else left but trust. Nothing about the process or about us feels favoured. We battle, like Job, to make sense of the darkness that has beset us. And whilst we battle despondency as we journey through the evening, the paradox is that when the evening comes, a new future is being prepared. Just as Israel had to leave Egypt at night, our transition has to be hidden from the enemy of our soul. The birthing of the purpose for our being favoured can only become visible once the invisible process of the "evening" has been finalised.

The reality of the evening in the change process addresses the fact that being favoured does not imply being shielded or exempted from the often dark realities of life.

Reality 2: The change process brings about a lonely place that will challenge our understanding of our significance over our understanding of our importance

Mark 4:36: "They had sent away the multitude."

Consider the spiritual physiognomy of the disciples from the following premise: The disciples were just ordinary men. Some were mere fishermen. They had almost no status or significance amongst people, but then Jesus chose them to walk with Him. This gave them the privilege of organising the crowds. At times they overstepped their boundaries, wanting to decide who should make contact with Jesus and who not. Their association with the miracle worker undoubtedly gave them a sense of power and importance. Suddenly they were confronted with a choice to leave behind that which made them feel powerful and important, the multitudes, as they had to send them away.

We observe from this passage (Mark 4:36) that the place of transition is a lonely one. Change cannot happen whilst we are in the midst of the multitudes. Every single person who made a great impact and had great influence on his or her generation experienced the lonely place of transition, be it Moses whilst wandering through the desert in search of purpose or be it Joseph chained in a prison in Egypt, doubting if his gift would ever be discovered. Let us not forget Jesus crying from a place of utter seclusion, "My God, my God why has Thou forsaken me?" I want to suggest that the lonely place of transition is needed if we are to achieve focus in relation to our bias predicate.[2] Being lonely during this phase brings into focus things otherwise invisible to us during the normal course of life. By no means is this an exciting position to be in. However, it does enlarge our understanding of what is significant (as opposed to what we used to see as important). Our willingness to let go of what appears important, like the disciples' willingness to send the multitudes away, will determine both the fluency and the success of our transition. At times, the favour placed on us requires a reconstruction of our environment. That is, a willingness to let go of the things which will hinder the full functioning of the favour with which we are blessed.

The reality of the lonely place during the change process poses the following question to us: "Do we understand our significance in the absence of others over our importance in their presence?" It thus teaches us that being favoured is not about being important; instead, it is about being significant.

Reality 3: The change process will bring us to places that defy logic and elicit a demand on our faith

Water

Making any form of transition brings with it a sense of uncertainty, an unpredictability that logic and reason often grapple with. Between the place where Jesus and the disciples were and the place where they had to go was nothing but water. The road from Egypt to the Promised Land was through the waters of the Jordan River. Jesus's earthly ministry started when He was submerged in the water of baptism. Every transition from the old to the new goes through water. Water is representative of the abstract, unknown patch we walk through in our pursuit of something new and fresh. It gives us an unfamiliar sinking feeling simply because we are used to the platform of dry land – logic and reason. What we know and what used to work become unresponsive in the new environment. The terms and conditions of the known become completely inadequate. And truthfully, we will not stop at conjuring up all sorts of plans to prevent our boat from sinking or capsizing, as it is only human instinct to do so. Putting forth our best effort, we would intensify our labour to keep above board. Mental and emotional fatigue gradually set in as the reality of our failed efforts starts to take its toll. It then dawns on us that our devices are "land-compatible", not "water-compatible". As the water environment brings us to the realisation that there are things beyond our control, it equally sets us up to become willing to search for One who is greater than what we are facing. The new environment, water, does not function on the basis of intellect or logic. Its economy is faith, the simple yet firm belief that God is there to take care of us. Once we engage the water environment with the right economy, i.e. faith, a sense of substance will begin to fill us.

The reality of the water environment produces in us the understanding that we are not just material beings but also spiritual beings. As favoured people, we often find ourselves in places and situations that defy logic, which places a demand on our faith.

Reality 4: The change process will test our consciousness of divine provision

---

Mark 4:35: "Let us pass over."

One of the dangers of being in transition is that during such a time, one can be subdued into becoming very self-centred. With the waves battering against our boat and with the potential prospect of our not making it through the storm, our battle becomes one of survival. Continually operating from survival mode could ultimately lead us to be sucked into the storm itself. As the space between us and the storm diminishes, we can, in a very subtle way, almost become part of the storm. Although our focus span is heightened during the change process, we do not necessarily focus on the things that matter or that could make a difference. We may find ourselves busy but not effective, surviving but not living. The juggling act of doing damage control, of keeping ourselves afloat amongst various things that could potentially sink us, can be mentally tiring. Possible help that is larger than life in almost ironic way is obscure from our vision as we battle to save ourselves.

The disciples in the scripture mentioned above did exactly that, failing to see the Help right next to them in the boat and so do we when we find ourselves in the heat of the change process. They did not understand that the different environment in which they had found themselves operated with a different economy. Before they left the shore on the other side, the instruction from Christ was clear but forgotten: "Let *us* pass over."

Christ accompanied His own instruction. It should be comforting to know that whilst He is the one assigning the passing over, the emphasis is really on "us". He never excludes Himself when He assigns us a task. We feel forsaken in the midst of the storm only because we are not conscious of His presence. The less conscious we are of God's presence, the more self-centred we become in our demeanour as we journey through rough patches. Selfishness is a mindset unconscious of the Provider.

Selfishness is a mindset unconscious of the Provider.

The reality of what we are conscious of is a test of what we are focused on. Being conscious of the higher order of provision will free us from selfishness during the change process.

Reality 5: The change process is divinely orchestrated, so it is one we cannot replicate at will

Mark 4:35: "Let us pass over."

Key to this verse is that the instruction to "pass over" to the other side emanated from Jesus. The disciples had very little knowledge of what was awaiting them. They were completely ignorant of the transition prepared for them. In *Principles of the Battlefield*, I write about the principle of the battle's being set. I basically convey the idea that the setting of the battle normally brings about a change in our environment, an environment that is immune to our decision-making power. Numerous biblical characters including Joseph, Job and Moses found themselves in this type of situation where things happened beyond their control, but those things had a much deeper purpose, one that they understood only later.

Such a time of transition is normally accompanied by a change in our environment. That is, something in our circumstances will change that is beyond our control. A moment of transition then presents itself, one planned and orchestrated by God. At the time of happenstance, we are of course not always aware of this reality. But the moment that besets us is always one we can never replicate or reconstruct ourselves. It is a "let us pass over" moment that is granted to us and that is directed at bringing us into a biased position, one driven and overseen by the Spirit of the Lord. Admittedly, when the "let us pass over" favour is being extended to us, we find that we have more questions than answers, as our perplexed understanding cannot decipher the course of things. A puzzle starts developing in our mind's eye, one administering equal doses of fear and curiosity. The moment has arrived. We dare not be timid and let the moment slide, as it is not within our power to recreate the moment with all its variables and constants.

Of course in the moment, it is very difficult for us to believe that what has befallen us is for our preservation. Such a time is normally one when things are not added to us but are taken away. Subtraction is a big part of the equation. We undergo a learning process, one that feels to be more about loss than about gain. But as contradictory as it may seem in the moment, God has our preservation at heart.

It was after such a process that Joseph declared to his brothers, "Now therefore be neither grieved nor angry with yourselves, that you sold me: for God *sent* me before you to preserve life" (Genesis 45:5). After the fact, Joseph's view of his transition period, during which he experienced betrayal, false accusations, and deception, was one of preservation. We may not always know or understand how it will all work out, but we can take courage from what seems to be a generic template when we look at the lives of men and women in scripture who kept on following God through the pass-over process.

The reality of having to make a transition is always divinely orchestrated and teaches us that the appearance of circumstances does not determine whether we are favoured or not. Such moments place a direct demand on our attention so that we focus on what we have been favoured with.

Reality 6: The change process is capable of causing motion within us

---

Mark 4:36: "Took him even as he was."

Very few things have such a powerful effect on our perception as does the change process. The change process has the ability to bend our perception as a furnace would precious metal. Perception is the golden lens through which we view God, ourselves, and the world. Going through a process of change undoubtedly challenges how we perceive things. During such a time, we normally change viewpoints on issues and subjects. We may make the comment, "I used to view the matter like this, but after what I have been through, I have changed my point of view." And such is the case because the change process is one that produces movement. It brings about cause and effect within us. It causes *turning* within us. For example, repentance as a change process causes us to *turn* inwardly towards God. The same is true of rebellion as a change process, as it also causes a *turning* within us, albeit a turn in a different direction. The issue we are facing, for argument's sake, may be a constant, but as we are *turned* during the change process, we end up perceiving it differently. Scripture teaches that with God, there, "is no variableness, neither no shadow of turning" (James 1:17). In short, He is unchangeable, "the same yesterday, today and forever" (Hebrews 13:8), because of His vantage point. He cannot be turned. But although He does not change, our perception of Him changes as we are being turned throughout the change process. And truthfully, our perception of the Lord may change either positively or negatively.

It was when an unexpected storm erupted in the lives of Job and his wife that his wife said, "Curse God and die."[3] Her response was related to how she had been turned in her perception of God. She could not find a way to stay with Job, because she deemed God untrustworthy. Job, however, was turned in a very different way and direction. In his final assessment, Job, after his difficult ordeal, attested that whereas he had once heard of the Lord, now he had seen Him.

The verse above reads that the disciples "took him [Jesus] even as he was". By extension, this means that when we approach the change process, we "take" the Lord with us into the situation as we understand Him to be. In other words, we enter with a certain level of faith in, and perception of,

God. But it is actually during the transition that we are being turned to see Him as *He is*. I think it is important to note that I am not implying here that the Lord will only reveal Himself to us in pressure situations. Neither do I subscribe to the idea that we have to go from one tough experience to the other to better understand the Lord. Rather, I'm arguing that we become more receptive to revelation during the change process. It is in the heat of what we face that our perception of the character of God is shaped.

Having an accurate versus an inaccurate understanding of God was the difference between characters such as Joseph and Saul, respectively, who were both favoured. Joseph, through his dreams and visions, understood that he had a great future, but he also comprehended being faithful to the giver of favour as essential to the operation of his favoured position. In private, he refused the advances of Potiphar's wife. Saul, on the other hand, although he was favoured, could not make the connection between his being favoured and having a healthy perception of the character of God. He despised the commandment of God. The difference between Joseph and Saul really came down to how they allowed their respective circumstances to shape their perception of God. In the text, the experience of the storm had a huge impact on the disciples' perception of Jesus. After He calmed the storm, they asked, "What manner of man is this?"

The change process will produce movement in us. Our perception of God's character is definitely not exempted from such movement. We cannot properly understand our bias predicate without having an accurate understanding of the giver of favour.

Reality 7: The change process will challenge our self-perception through what happens *in us* rather than what happens *to us*

Mark 4:38: "Master carest thou not that we perish?"

In Mark 4, the focus of the disciples gradually shifts from the storm to themselves. They had almost given up on wanting to save anything else but their lives. The storm became something they could do little about. Their efforts proved too weak to salvage what they had with them on the boat. The storm outside became the storm inside them. Not only is our perception of God's character challenged during the change process, but so is our perception of our own worth.

In the materialistic world in which our generation lives, money and status appear to have become the gauge of our worth. Such an avaricious system inevitably leads to an overemphasis on the role of money – hence the culture where we try to shop and dress our uncertainties away and yet remain uncertain of our true worth. We are sometimes even fooled into thinking that occupying a position of status will give us a better sense of worth. If only we climb the ladder higher and faster, then some of our uncertainties and doubts will go away. In the end, we discover only that all our inner uncertainties increase once we reach our goal. And the reality is this: unless we change the yardstick we use to measure our worth, we will never achieve a different outcome.

A change (hopefully for the better) in how we view ourselves is an enormously important miracle. In fact, how we view ourselves is a miracle that sustains all other miracles. It is also an important element in the continual work of favour (or destruction). We see this principle throughout scripture. In the Garden of Eden, for example, the tree of knowledge of good and evil was there all the time, but it was not always an issue. Most of what satan did during the temptation of Eve was to change Eve's perception of the tree. As soon as she had perceived it differently, she reacted without duress and ate of it. We also witness this principle when Jesus rose from the grave. The first miracle He performed thereafter involved a change of perception. The scriptures record the miracle as follows: "And He opened their understanding" (Luke 24:45). The learned refer to this as a paradigm shift in thinking.

Joseph, after being betrayed, sold as a slave, falsely accused, and imprisoned, had the following view of all that had happened to him: "For God had sent me before you." Had he clung to the idea of being sold by men and not sent by God, the outcome between him and his brothers would have been different. It was this perception that kept his understanding of his worth intact. Our perception of our worth is not so much influenced by what happens *to us* as it is by what happens *in us* when we go through the change process. This holds especially true when there is a mismatch between our outer circumstances and our belief of being favoured by the Lord.

The reality of the change process will challenge what happens *in* us rather than what happens *to* us. Our self-perception during the change process will be heavily confronted, as there will not necessarily be a correlation between the circumstances we find ourselves in and our being favoured by the Lord.

Reality 8: The change process will challenge our knowing that we matter

Mark 4:38: "Master carest thou not that we perish?"

The question the disciples are posing here has little to do with the storm. It is a question that concentrates on the disciples' value and position. At the heart of difficulty, and in the heat of battle, we often are stripped to the point of asking only this one question: "Master, carest Thou not that we perish?" We can paraphrase this question in the following ways: "Who am I to You, Lord?" and "How much do I mean to You, Lord?" This question goes beyond the storm. It is, in fact, a question of love, a question which, in the end, becomes even more important than the storm itself. Going beyond the drama, scandals, or losses of the storm, this question draws us to experience peace and calm after all our tiring attempts not to sink. We want to know how much we mean to the Lord. We want to know how much we matter, if at all.

I have never been a proponent of the type of Christian experience wherein a person endlessly swings between being in trouble and then being rescued by God. Still, something very peculiar happens to us when we are up against hardship. We are forced into spiritual places we would otherwise not naturally drift into. We ask questions we would not otherwise ask. It is easy to understand our importance, but not necessarily easy to understand that we matter, when the sun shines. The change process has the ability to force us to question our worth.

In the verse mentioned above, the disciples reach a point where they are forced to ask this question, but only through what they perceive as non-action on the part of Jesus (i.e. He is sleeping). It was this perceived non-action that drove them to ask the question, "Don't You care?" In the midst of any change process, we are ultimately forced into a stocktaking of what God did or did not do. Based on our assessment of what He (normally) did not do and of what, in our understanding, He should have done, we conclude that we don't really matter. It is the perceived non-action on the part of the Lord that brings us into the mental feebleness of thinking that He does not care. Caring, in our logic, would mean action on His part, which we would subsequently interpret that we matter. Whenever we perceive non-action on the part of God, the equation of whether or not we matter breaks apart and defies our logic. The search for whether we matter or not then gets pushed into a realm where logic is broken. In John 11, we see this sense of disappointment when Martha perceives Jesus as having not acted, as He arrived after Lazarus had died. Martha is quoted as saying, "Lord, if you had been here, my brother would not have died" (John 11:21). Martha is implying non-action on the part of Jesus.

I suggest that what we sometimes perceive as non-action on the part of the Lord means one of two things, though these are easier to see in the aftermath of the storm:

- The Lord wants us to know that we will be fine and that we should not stop believing whilst in the midst of our change process. Hence after Jesus had calmed the storm, He rebuked the disciples for having little faith.
- The Lord has a greater miracle in store for us.

> Martha told Jesus up front that He had failed to act and that now He was too late. His being late did not mean that the situation was lost. It only meant that the miracle would be greater.

A vital truth is revealed to us in the way the message of Lazarus's illness is conveyed to Jesus:

"The one whom you love is sick" (John 11:3).

Our worth and position ("the one whom you love") always supersedes our condition ("is sick"). In short, we matter above and beyond our circumstances.

The reality of the change process will challenge our knowing that we matter. We should have an understanding of the functioning of God's love, as that forms the basis for our being favoured.

In conclusion, what we perceive as our world falling apart is, rather, the change process, orchestrated by the One who favours us, fragmenting the world we live in. This initially brings about a discrepancy between our outer reality and our knowing that the Lord has favoured us for a particular task. This is a crucial, although sometimes a painful, process, as the heart of the process is about aligning us closer to the Lord, who has favoured and chosen us. As favoured people, we cannot be effective in this world unless we understand the One who has called us out of this world to live in this world.

"For He has regarded the lowly state of His maidservant" (Luke 1:48).

Summary of Chapter 2

1. Talent and a gifting is the prerogative of the Lord, but aligning ourselves to such grace is our responsibility as humans.

2. Having created a being in His "image and after His likeness", God has opted for a collaboration between Divinity and humanity as an operating model.

3. There are eight generic realities to the change process. These are as follows:

    *   Through the change process, we learn that being favoured does not imply being shielded or exempted from the often dark realities of life.
    *   The change process brings about a lonely place that will challenge our understanding of our significance over our understanding of our importance.
    *   The changes process will bring us to places that defy logic and elicit a demand on our faith.
    *   The change process will test our consciousness of divine provision.
    *   The change process, divinely orchestrated, is not one we can replicate at will.
    *   The change process is capable of causing motion within us.
    *   The change process will challenge our self-perception through what happens in us rather than what happens to us.

- The change process will challenge our knowing that we matter.

4. Selfishness is a mindset unconscious of the Provider.

5. Favoured people cannot properly understand their bias predicate without understanding the giver of favour.

6. Evidence of God's caring, according to our logic, would mean action on God's part.

7. Whenever we perceive non-action on the part of God, the equation of whether or not we matter breaks apart and defies our logic.

CHAPTER 3

IF I AM FAVOURED, WHY DON'T I THINK SO?

> He has scattered the proud in the imagination
> of their heart.
>
> Luke 1:51

> For you are no longer thinking simply about
> right and wrong; you are trying to catch the
> good infection from a Person. It is more like
> painting a portrait than like obeying a set of
> rules.
>
> C. S. Lewis

Mary is contemplating by herself the recent visitation by the angel of the Lord. The divine event has never left her imagination. Repeatedly in her mind, she revisits that celestial moment. That heaven and earth collided in her is beyond her comprehension. Being favoured by the Lord for such an eternal purpose is a grace too marvellous for her to envision. The words of the angel ricochet in her head daily. Being impregnated by the work of the Holy Spirit has brought an inexplicable excitement to her life. She sometimes catches herself smiling and giggling uncontrollably, like a teenage girl in love. But there is also a web of thoughts, fluctuating between excitement and fear, eliciting a conflict inside her. How does she share the excitement of such a reality with a world not amenable to it? How does she share it with Joseph? A silent, underlying anxiety floods her soul as she considers the various possible scenarios once she breaks the news to Joseph and her close friends. She is untameably desperate, wanting to publicise the latest unfolding in her life, but she realises that the conscious paradigm of her community may not be accepting.

Nazareth is a very small town in which gossip can spread like wildfire. It is an archetypal small town with a dual nature. On the one hand, Nazareth gives off a family-like impression, but on the other hand, the everybody-knows-everybody's-business ethos can be as lethal as a weapon of mass destruction. Mary has witnessed countless occasions when the deadly poison of the tongue, through gossip and negativity, crushed the image and spirit of many people in Nazareth. The moral fibre of this little town is as unadulterated as mother's milk. Anything threatening the breakdown of morality is treated with austerity and utmost disgust.

What if the town were to discover that she is pregnant, but not with Joseph's child? "What will the community think of me?" she wonders. "What is the image that my relatives will have of me?" she wonders. Her "infidelity" would be the talk of the town – and of her sweet, innocent image, nothing would be left. She will not be able to prove the divine encounter, she realises. Although not beset by guilt, she is in no position to defend her innocence. The controversy of emotions and the sense of divine chaos are utterly debilitating as her imagination runs riot on her. The possibility that Joseph will want to leave her is also not completely out of the question in her mind. Yet amidst these tranquillity-disturbing thoughts, there is a silent but strong confidence floating through her mind. The thoughts appear to glide at a level that is shallow compared to the deep-seated change that Mary is experiencing. The change in how she views herself feels bottomless. A different picture of herself hangs on the walls of her imagination. The old, inferior view of herself is progressively dimming. She is still the same Mary, still living in Nazareth, but immovable movement has happened in her imagination. "If God calls me 'highly favoured', then I must be someone," she argues. "I must matter," she concludes. As her focus is bonded to the deep-seated shift in her imagination, it dawns on her that all her fears are in relation to people: what they might say, what they might think, and what will become of her if they don't accept or understand. As much as she cannot explain why she had been chosen, she cannot make people believe or understand her divine encounter. The true impact of what has happened to her is too divine and implausible to verbalise.

Mary is starting to formulate the conclusion that what God says about a person, and what the person says to him or herself, ultimately determines that person's self-image. "Strong as the opinions of people might be, they should never be foundational," Mary reminds herself. Mary cannot offer any reason or excuse for her being visited by favour. The visitation of grace came unrequested. Amidst the restraint of the political atmosphere, and amidst the religious legalism, a newly sculpted image of herself has emerged in her heart. The entrance of divine favour has moulded in her a new perception of herself. The footprints of the old perception are gradually being blown away by the winds of favour.

In her mind, Mary has hints that there must be a bigger picture to all that has happened to her, a picture she cannot quite put together herself. Like her contemporaries, she has only ever had the understanding and expectation that the coming Messiah would overthrow the Roman Empire. And now, still in disbelief, she is carrying the child on whose shoulders that hope rests. How it is going to happen and where it is going to unfold, she does not know. But for now, she is content. It is a liberating reality. She thinks differently about herself, sees life in new dimensions, and has the unshakeable understanding that God is personal. Just as she is starting to revel in her newfound freedom, the thought of how Joseph will react to the news seems to slam on the brakes. Although still there, the thought has lost its accompanying anxiety, as Mary has come to the critical realisation that what God has started, He must be able to conclude. For now, she has decided to allow herself the full experience of the shift in her imagination.

* * *

Why is a discussion of the imagination important to the triangular interworking of our being favoured, our having been chosen, and our having been assigned a purpose? I suggest that it is important because our being chosen for whatever purpose starts in the mind of God. In receiving and fulfilling any choosing or purpose, our own mind must be receptive to the mind of God. If our mind, in particular our imagination, is not conducive to receiving the picture that God has of our lives, then we cannot be receptive to any choosing or purpose. Through the functioning of the mind,[1] we perceive, conceive of, and shape our lives. Our understanding of the mind's function and its linkage to what has been gifted to us thus becomes vital in our pursuit of living out our purpose and fulfilling our choosing. How and what we think should thus matter to us as it does to God.

The functioning of the imagination

I still remember a very dark time my family and I faced. It was probably one of our biggest battles, one of those stubborn ones that lasts not a month or two, but six or seven years. During that time, the pendulum swung for the umpteenth time between a mirage of the end and deep levels of despair and hopelessness. And as it is with these sorts of battles, the negativity and bad energy became relentless. Not only did I get drawn into the battle, but also I drew the battle, with all its negativity, into my soul. Towards the later part of that six-to seven-year period, I fell into a very deep depression. I sunk deeper and deeper into a bottomless pit of despair as each day passed. I recall that I felt successful during those days when I merely made it through the day without making an attempt on my life.

During that time, I read an article in a newspaper about a renowned singer who had committed suicide. According to the article, the man took his life whilst he was surrounded by Bible verses and scripture readings. His reasons, according to the newspaper article, for committing suicide were not that different from the circumstances we had found ourselves in at that time. The article left me cold and despondent, and gave me the feeling that I too was being led to the "abattoir". I remember the resounding question in my mind: "What makes you think that you are going to make it?" Gripped by palpable fear, I realised I needed help – and I needed it fast. Help arrived shortly thereafter in this form:

> "And God saw that the wickedness of man was great in the earth, and that every *imagination* of the thoughts of his *heart* was only evil continually" (Genesis 6:5, emphasis added).

This passage of scripture gives us an almost slow motion view of the dynamics involved in the processes of the mind. Through the years, we have learnt that there is a direct linkage between the heart and the thoughts, and that in attempting to guard our heart, it is imperative to guard our thoughts. But the dynamic of the imagination has always been omitted from this equation. The imagination is the part of the mind that produces a picture to accompany every thought. Guarding our imagination thus becomes an integral part of keeping our thoughts and heart intact. Any thought without an accompanying picture is like a portrait without a picture – meaningless, powerless.

We think in pictures. During the temptation, satan could not just promise Jesus the kingdoms of the world and tempt Him to worship him. He had to take Jesus to a high mountain to "*show* unto Him all the kingdoms of the world in a moment of time" (Luke 4:5, emphasis added). Joseph's dreams were God's way of imprinting onto his imagination an indelible image of his destiny. We can thus recognise the necessity of the imagination to both the destructive (through temptation) and the fulfilment (i.e. fulfilling our choosing and purpose) processes.

By way of the verse in Genesis 6:5, we can explain the functioning between the imagination, the thoughts, and the heart as follows:

- The imagination is the faculty where we paint the picture. It functions as the entry point to the mind.
- The thoughts are the faculty where we find expression for what we see.
- The heart is the faculty where we find motive and reason to execute what we have seen.

The imagination remains the entry point to our heart, the place where we, as artists of our own lives, carve and chisel the image to be moulded. From the meaning of the word "imagination", we get an understanding of the imagination's importance to the functioning of the processes of the mind. The root word of "imagination" is "image". The Hebrew word for imagination is the word "Yaw-tsar"[2], which means, "to mould into a form especially as a potter". The fact that the imagination is capable of being moulded gives the impression that it has capacity, which is a prerequisite for ability. Both the destructive and fulfilment processes, if they are to be successful, are reliant on the ability of the imagination to be moulded. The capacity for any process is built in the imagination first. What we allow to take shape in our imagination will manifest as an image in our reality. If the "sketch factory" produces distorted pictures, then the fabrication of our reality will likewise be distorted. Although we have very little control over the influx of images entering the imagination, we do have control over which images we send on to the heart for production.

We want to live our lives at harvest level- i.e.
we want to enjoy the fruit of what we produce
through the imagination – but we want to do
the management thereof at seed level,
i.e. in the imagination.

David serves as an example of someone who understood the dynamics and linkage between the imagination, the thoughts, and the heart. When the people were praising and worshipping the Lord, David prayed the following:

"Oh Lord, God of Abraham, Isaac, and of Israel, our father keep this forever in the *imagination* of *the thoughts* of *the heart* of your people" (1 Chronicles 29:18, emphasis added).

He prayed this prayer using the exact order that God had mentioned in Genesis 6:5: "the imagination of the thoughts of the heart". Could it perhaps be that he had learnt the dynamics and linkage between the imagination, the thoughts, and the heart through his ordeal with Bathsheba? Did he perhaps learn from the horrific consequences of sending the wrong picture into his heart for production?

The seed of the imagination is also the seat of authority

What we define as our choosing and purpose is, in fact, God's picture, which becomes the seed for our lives.

A fundamental part of our having been created in the image and likeness of God is that of free will, which requires a free and independent mind. From this premise we have the ability to create. The imagination, as part of the mind, allows us to exercise our freedom and independent mind. To have freedom is to have authority and control, in particular over one's mind. I believe that the account of the demonic Gadarene, as recorded in Mark 15, is of particular interest in this regard. After Jesus had healed the Gadarene and had broken the demoniac powers that held him captive, the people were afraid and amazed because they found him to be in "his right mind". By implication, this means that he previously had no control or authority over his life, as the demonic powers had taken control of his mind. Through having exerted control over his mind, the demonic powers were also in charge of the paintbrush and crayons of his imagination. He was tortured day and night because those demonic forces had access to the walls of his imagination. The Gadarene was found to be in his right mind after Jesus healed him because he had regained control over his mind and, thus, over his life. He could live again, have freedom again, make independent decisions (such as wanting to go with Jesus) again, and exercise a degree of self-governance again. Such was the case, I believe, because the mind is the seat of authority in a person, and imagination is the smallest seed form of the mind. We can equate the imagination to a cell, i.e. the smallest component in the make-up of the human body. In cases such as cancer, the breakdown of the body starts at the smallest level. In likening the imagination to a cell in the human body, we can almost describe the imagination as the smallest component in the make-up of our lives. Both the destruction and build-up of our lives starts with the smallest component: our imagination. Scripture declares, "As he thinks in his heart, so is he" (Proverbs 23:7). We cannot build purposeful lives if we cling to old, destructive pictures. Being favoured demands that we change the pictures that are hung on the walls of our imagination, if those pictures are not compatible to our purpose. We want to live our lives at harvest level – i.e. we want to enjoy the fruit of what we produce through the imagination – but we want to do the management thereof at seed level, i.e. in the imagination.

Our mind cannot operate in any other way as we take after God our Creator. Throughout the entire Genesis creation account, we see the pattern of God's having had a picture and then, through words, giving utterance and allowance to those pictures, thereby bringing them into reality. We learn from the creation account that the seed of the imagination is the path that everything invisible follows to crystallisation. Our mind, our thoughts, and their accompanying pictures are intimate and very personal to us. The mind is the most private part of any person, a part that can only be shared through choice, as it cannot be seen with the naked eye. "Opening up" to someone necessitates a sharing of our thoughts. The very same holds true for God. When God shares His thoughts for us, He is sharing an intimate part of Himself with us. The Lord does not just want to share a favour with us; He favours us in sharing His thoughts with us. Christ came not only to shed His precious blood for us, but also to share His most intimate self with us by giving us His mind (1 Corinthians 2:16).

The capacity for any process is built in the imagination first.

The following scripture is a prime example of God's opening the curtains over His thoughts:

> "For I know the thoughts that I think toward you, says the Lord, thoughts of peace and not evil to give you an expected end" (Jeremiah 29:11).

Here we see not only the thoughts of God, thoughts of "peace and not evil", but also the accompanying picture, "an expected end". He wants to place our entire lives inside His picture frame. God's thoughts do not cover only the inception of our lives; they also stretch to our end, an expected end. The psalmist had an overwhelming moment when he ran into the thoughts of God. He proclaimed,

> "How precious are your thoughts unto me, O God! How great is the sum of them! If I should count them they are more in number than the sand" (Psalm 139:17–18).

What we understand as our choosing and purpose is really God sharing an intimate part of Himself with us:

His thoughts and imagination. It is when we do come into contact with God's picture of, and thoughts for, our lives that we become imbued with a sense of purpose and calling. If God's thoughts are "more than the sand", then this implies that God is never out of thoughts for anyone's life. Hence no person on earth can ever be born without purpose. God's picture for our lives is our authority. It is the point of our being favoured, our bias predicate. It is when we submit ourselves to God and align the picture of our imagination to God's purpose for our lives that we gain control over the seat of authority and, thus, over our lives.

We are favoured because we have been handed a picture from God's imagination concerning us. If the picture in our imagination is not linked to the one in God's imagination, then we can never fulfil our choosing and purpose. Hence we have been given weapons for "casting down imaginations" (2 Corinthians 10:5), for defending His picture against the walls of our imagination.

The imagination serves as a mirror

The picture in our imagination serves as a mirror that informs us of whether we are following our choosing and purpose or not.

The body part we mostly refer to when defining our identity is the face. Yet the face is the body part we ourselves can't see. We need the help of a mirror to see our face. Most of us would not dare to leave our house without taking a look in the mirror. As far as our imagination is concerned, it serves as a mirror to show the quality of our outer reality.

We are image-beings that function from the inside out. In [3]*The Seven Habits of Highly Effective People,* Steven R. Covey makes a wonderful point, stating that all things are created twice: first in the mind and then in the material world. This is one of those principles that operate daily in our lives. In fact, creation came about through this principle. The importance of this principle is that it enables us to measure failure and/or success. Without a picture in the imagination of what success or failure would look like, we would not be able to do a measure thereof. A match between our mental picture and what manifests in our physical reality produces fulfilment, or satisfaction. A deviation obviously brings about dissatisfaction. When Adam discovered that he was naked, he knew that intention and reality no longer corresponded. Hence, in the Garden of Eden, God and Adam knew that a fall, a deviation, had taken place after Adam and Eve partook of the forbidden fruit.

The purpose for being favoured is to bring about a correspondence between our outer reality and the picture sketched on the walls of our imagination. The visitation of favour will never leave us without a picture of the task we are chosen for. Abraham had the picture of the stars in heaven and the sand of the earth as a reference. Joseph had a dream. Moses knew he was deliverer of the Israelites from the Egyptians, and Jesus endured the cross because of the "joy that was set before Him" (Hebrews 5:2). We are never chosen without being handed a picture of our purpose. God said to Joshua (Joshua 1:8) that if he meditated (created a mental picture) on the Word, he would have great success, as the physical manifestation would always follow the mental picture.

Bringing what we have seen imprinted on our imagination to fruition is the difference amongst what James called "doers and hearers of the Word" (James 1:25). James describes a hearer of the Word as someone who, upon seeing his face in a mirror, walks away and forgets how he looks. Unless we capture what we see imprinted in our imagination, we will walk through life without knowing ourselves and with no sense of identity, choosing, or purpose. In other words, we will be faceless. Through being favoured, we bridge the gap between our choosing and our purpose; we perceive in our imagination what manifests in our physical reality. If we don't, then our entire inner atmosphere becomes a breeding ground of frustration and friction. Hence we have the phenomenon of people who have almost every material thing their hearts desire and yet who feel like failures. Looking at their perceived outside success, we find it difficult to understand why they feel like failures. And the difficulty in understanding this arises from the fact that we don't have insight into the picture in their imagination from which they have deviated.

The importance of a discussion on the imagination in relation to our being favoured and chosen is exactly this: our being chosen is in relation to a specific purpose, the successful outcome of which is communicated in the imagination first. The same holds true for the destructive process through temptation. The direction of the process happens by the same functioning – by the *imagination of the thoughts of the heart*. Scripture says that the devil walks around as a "roaring lion seeking whom he can devour" (1 Peter 5:8). Seeking implies a calculated risk or opportunity. The calculated risk that the enemy is taking, I suggest, is in relation to the mind, where the picture painted on the walls of the imagination is broken – through unforgiveness, hurt, unresolved disappointment, rejection, dissatisfaction, bitterness, etc. – in order to strike a potential successful match for the temptation. When the mirror is broken or cracked, we simply cannot see our purpose or ourselves.

In our not understanding what we are fighting
for or against, God, in our distorted opinion,
becomes our next best opponent.

The first image that was engraved in Adam's imagination must have been God's face, or so I believe. For Adam to have received the breath of God through his nostrils, God must have been very close to Adam. Adam knew who he was because of the mirror into which he looked: God's face. I believe that all is not lost when the walls of our imagination have been defiled through hurt, past pain, abuse, etc. When we seek the Lord's face, the mirror of our imagination can be restored so we can regain a clear vision of our purpose.

The variable for success, whether in the destructive process or the fulfilment process, is the inner picture in the imagination we pursue and maintain.

The imagination serves as a link to faith

Protecting the picture in our imagination will keep our faith alive, which is essential to producing our calling.

The clearest definition that we have of faith is found in Hebrews 11:1, "Now faith is the substance of the things hoped for." From this definition, we can deduce that faith and hope cannot function in isolation. The one functions as a result of the other. Hope, in simple terms, is an ideal picture of a certain situation. That ideal picture is needed for faith to function. When we do lose sight of pursuing that picture, we become directionless, lose belief, and have no reason to act in faith.

When we break through to form an understanding of our choosing and purpose, an ensuing battling is almost unavoidable. That battle is referred to in scripture as the "good fight of faith".

> "Fight the good fight of faith" (1 Timothy 6:12).

> "I have fought the good fight I have finished the race, I have kept the faith" (2 Timothy 4:7).

Seeing that the operation of faith is inseparable from the picture created by hope, an attack by the enemy of our soul on our faith thus has to be launched at the picture of hope, which resides in the imagination. Where hope is eroded, faith becomes static. Producing what has been placed in us does not (in most cases) happen under normal circumstances. Instead, it requires stressful and high-pressure situations, which require faith to be present. Normally during such situations, which are usually divinely orchestrated, we find it difficult to decipher their intended purpose, which is to help pull out of us what has been placed inside of us.

This is normally the time when we start focussing on the external circumstances whilst losing sight of the imprint of the picture in our imagination. Then, instead of correctly allowing the external circumstances to help pull out of us our choosing and purpose, we pull the atmosphere of the circumstances (negativity, doubt, impossibility, etc.) into our mind. We then successfully blur the line between our circumstances and the fight of faith. In a strange way, we also become confused about who our real enemy is. And in our not understanding what we are fighting for or against, God, in our distorted opinion, becomes our next best opponent.

There may be many kinds of circumstances, but there is only one battle: the good fight of faith. In part, the battle of faith entails protecting the picture in our imagination that enables us to run our race. Anyone who loses the battle of faith loses him- or herself. Not losing faith is the essence of everything we face. We may sometimes lose cars, houses, jobs, and even loved ones, but in the midst of our losses we can never afford to lose faith. We can afford any loss or disappointment if our faith remains intact, but all our gains and achievements without faith equate to a loss of ourselves. Faith is the fence around the picture of our being highly favoured that is engraved on our imagination; the restart button for a failed and bruised life; the first step towards, and the road to, our destiny; the fail-safe mechanism to the adventurous spirit; and the breath of highly favoured people.

The story of David and Goliath serves as an important illustration of this principle (in my book *Principles of the Battlefield*, I elaborate on this point). By the time David entered the battlefield, Saul and his men had experienced a challenge from Goliath for forty consecutive days. By then they were thoroughly scared. Saul and his men had successfully pulled the atmosphere of the situation – fear, doubt, etc. – into their minds. When David arrived on the scene, he pitched battle, uncontaminated by the external situation. He entered the battle with no weapons, as he was just the cheese-boy. But he did enter the battle with an unadulterated imagination, one in which the picture of hope was undamaged and the linkage to faith was exceptionally strong. Only two things moved David into battling Goliath: he was in covenant with God, and he had an indelible picture in his imagination of killing the bear and the lion for the sake of the sheep. Saul and his men had neither of these things at the time. It was that picture that gave David the edge of faith to basically conclude that what had happened to the bear and the lion would happen to Goliath. Saul and his men stood there in fear, possibly because of their past failures. Their imaginations did not hold the right linkage between hope and the fight.

I previously alluded to the fact that the imagination can be moulded. As a result thereof, it has the capacity to carry the potential for future purpose and past failures alike. Unfortunately we cannot carry our past failures and future purpose at equal measure. Paul communicates an important point in dealing with the past when he writes the following:

> "but one thing I do, forgetting those things which are behind and reaching forward to those things which are ahead" (Philippians 3:13).

I don't believe that "forgetting those things which are behind" is meant to indicate a memory loss or a denial of the past, as we can neither completely forget nor deny the past. When we look closely at this verse, we see that "forgetting" is contrasted against "reaching forward". We see here the reciprocal relationship between our thoughts (particularly our imagination because we also remember in pictures) and our actions. I suggest that what Paul is advocating here is for us to start reaching forward towards a new purpose whilst we are *in the midst* of a past that is trying to pull us into its atmosphere. There is no pause period between the past's conclusion and the new purpose's commencement. The "reaching forward" has to happen whilst the past is still trying to force itself upon our imagination. Reaching forward would mean that our mental environment would start following our actions and vice versa. The past will gradually fade as we reach out to lay claim of the new picture that is starting to break through our imagination. It becomes a continuous walk. We start making inroads into the old picture of past pain and hurt as we start extrapolating purpose from that pain by reaching forward. As was the case with Joseph throughout his continuous walk against the grain of pain, he gave the picture of his purpose a chance over his woeful past.

The picture we have in our imagination, of our purpose and our having been chosen, deserves a chance over whatever dreadful past we may have experienced. Through faith, God establishes those who are favoured in the imagination of the thoughts of their hearts.

"He has scattered the proud in the imagination of their heart" (Luke 1:51).

Summary of Chapter 3

1. We cannot guard our thoughts and heart effectively unless we guard our imagination.

2. The imagination is the faculty where we paint the picture. It functions as the entry point to the mind.

3. The thoughts are the faculty where we find expression for what we see.

4. The heart is the faculty where we find motive and reason to execute what we have seen.

5. There is a vast difference between our circumstances and the battle we fight.

6. There are many different kinds of circumstances, but there is only one battle: the good fight of faith.

7. The seed of the imagination is also the seat of authority.

8. The imagination serves as a mirror.

9. The imagination serves as a link to faith.

10. We can afford any loss or disappointment if our faith remains intact, but all our gains and achievements without faith equate to a loss of ourselves.

CHAPTER 4

IF I AM FAVOURED, WHY DON'T
I KNOW MY PURPOSE?

Let it be to me according to Your Word.

Luke 1:38

In pursuing our spiritual journey, we need to be clear about the goal. The spiritual life does not consist in self-realization but in the vision of God.

Eddie Gibbs and Ian Coffey

Mary understands intuitively that the time has come to inform Joseph of her pregnancy. She is not sure that she has the courage to convey this to him, but she realises that the situation is one that can speak for itself. If she does not tell Joseph, the signs from her body will. She is left with no choice but to reveal to him the truth, a truth she is not sure how he will react to. There is a noticeable anxiety in her voice as she gets ready to tell Joseph. The palms of her hands feel sweaty and her body shaky as she breaks the news to him. Joseph's countenance is sufficiently ambiguous for Mary not to draw any sort of conclusion about what he is thinking.

There is a blank stare in his expression. He was not prepared for this; nothing could have prepared him for such news. "This is completely outrageous," Joseph thinks to himself as a sense of betrayal grips his mind. Mary's being pregnant is difficult enough for Joseph to accept, let alone the idea that this has come about by way of some "divine force". Joseph is a realist, a pragmatic man, a carpenter. He finds Mary's explanation impossible to comprehend. The look in his eyes signals the fact that he cannot work around this in his head, as he is faced with believing the unbelievable, accepting the inconceivable, and trusting beyond the natural.

Mary cannot prove anything of what she has said to Joseph. The very foundation of their relationship suddenly feels shaken. "In no way can I build a future with the woman I love on illusions," Joseph thinks. How would he be able to reconcile himself to such an illogical situation, a situation contorted in suspicion? He feels confused and anxious, and he finds himself wanting to divorce this surreal event. Joseph questions Mary's motives for "dragging" God into her "shame". He knows Mary as someone who epitomises integrity and truth, but the current set of indigestible circumstances inevitably engages him in trying to figure out who the "other man" could be. He carefully considers days and times when Mary had been away from home. Her last visit to Elizabeth particularly begs his attention. Elizabeth has always been dear to Mary, but that visit was Mary's first visit to Elizabeth that lasted for three consecutive months. The "idea" that she is pregnant with the Saviour of the world by the Holy Spirit coincides with her last visit to Elizabeth. "The other man has to be there. Where else?" Joseph reasons with himself.

A few weeks have passed now. Mary cannot shake the feeling that Joseph is slipping away from her. Joseph longs for the normality they used to have. It is unclear whether he wants to be part of this new abnormality. He comes across as vague and distant. Mary feels powerless, as she cannot vindicate herself by pointing to the facts of the situation. Never before has she had to deal with a truthful situation that she has been unable to prove. Yet in the midst of all of this uncertainty, Mary feels propelled by divine appointment. She remembers the words she had spoken as her only reply to the message from the angel: "Let it be according to Your Word." She is being driven and carried by that reply. In the interim, Joseph, after careful consideration, has concluded that he is not prepared to live with the contradiction. He has been through the scenario innumerable times and has been in the balance of equally loving Mary and wanting to walk out on her. But Mary has become one with the situation, so the only way he can divorce the situation is to divorce himself from her. Joseph is completely convinced about the direction he has to take. In his mind, he shuts the door on Mary and on the "unknown" child.

Mary, on the other hand, is still silently hoping that Joseph will warm to the idea. "Once the reality has set in, he will become enthused about the whole situation," Mary keeps telling herself. Unbeknownst to Mary, Joseph, in the morning, will disappear silently and divorce her and the child.

But that night in a dream, an angel appears to Joseph, instructing him, "Don't separate from Mary. She is pregnant with the hope of the world." Joseph awakes not just from sleep but also, with fear and trembling, to the realisation that in his wanting to separate from Mary, he was actually planning on walking out on God. He grasps that the situation dressed in contradiction and inexplicability has, all along, been divinely charged. Overwhelmed by a sense purpose, Joseph tries to come to terms with the vastness of his responsibility. "No wonder, although he thought Mary was insane she was never inconsistent in her version of the divine ordeal" Joseph thinks to himself. He is not sure where all of this is leading to, but he has found a preparedness to trust God's motive and a willingness to follow it. Just as Mary, he was chosen. He must stay with Mary; he must protect the baby. The sense of *must* that he feels does not make him feel as if his free will is being infringed upon. Rather, it gives him a sense of purpose and direction.

* * *

I don't think the concept of purpose is necessarily an easy one to break down. For some of us, our purpose is not necessarily doing one single thing all our lives. Instead, it is doing something for a season before we move on to do something else. Sometimes our functional evolution allows for the notion of sub-assignments that are part of one holistic purpose. Technically, God has only one purpose, which every other purpose we may have or discover flows from and to. That single purpose is recoded as follows:

> "You are worthy, O Lord ... for you have created
> all things, and for your pleasure they are and
> were created" (Revelation 4:11).

What we define as our own purpose is technically an assignment aligned with that single purpose. For His pleasure, the sum of our personal lives is meant to be an extension of that single purpose. For the sake of this discussion, I will use the words "purpose" and "assignment(s)" interchangeably.

We can never quite understand why and how God chooses us for certain assignments. And it is so that the recipient of the purpose at times struggles more with the calling and the task than the spectators do. It is most definitely not an easy process from the inception of our choosing and purpose to the acceptance thereof, when we declare, "Let it be according to Your Word." The in-between is normally marked by a misunderstanding of what we want versus what God has in mind – i.e. our will versus His. It is a space where we may become suspicious of God's motives, as the short-term direction of our lives appears contrary to what we had in mind for ourselves. Yet during such times, the sense of purpose that has been birthed within us propels us beyond the forces that resist us. As we become heavy with purpose, we will inevitably experience all sorts of resistance. In an earlier chapter, we learnt that divine favour does not function outside the confines of purpose.

There are a number of truths we should keep in mind when dealing with the concept of purpose in relation to our being chosen.

Purpose chooses us and not us it

Jesus, during one of His conversations with His disciples, made this important statement: "You did not choose me, I chose you." Purpose always chooses us and not us it. In Galatians 1:15–16, Paul expresses the idea of being chosen as follows: "But when it pleased God, who separated me from my mother's womb, and called me by His grace to reveal His Son in me." We are not chosen because we are favoured; rather, we are favoured because we are chosen. Divine favour serves as the catalyst to prepare the environment for purpose to function in. Like it was for Mary, purpose impregnates us and not vice versa. We are merely benefactors of being chosen. God has always just been looking for a vessel. Purpose is birthed by our coming into contact with God's choice for our lives, as was the case for Mary and Joseph. They were chosen before they knew it. When God's choice for them was manifested to them, they came into contact with it – and purpose was birthed in their hearts. The same was true for David. Whilst being behind the sheep, he was chosen, but he was yet to come into contact with God's choice. On the day he did come into contact with that choice, purpose was birthed in his heart. Whilst Saul was persecuting members of the Christian church, he stumbled upon God's choice for his life and found purpose in his heart. When we stumble upon God's choice for our lives, purpose is birthed in our hearts. It is our choosing that gives us a sense a purpose. We cannot choose our own purpose. It chooses us as we draw near to God and come into contact with His choice for our lives.

Purpose seeks surrender

The idea that purpose chooses us and not us it in itself will elicit some form of conflict within us. God did choose to create us as beings with an independent free will, yet, as with everything God does, He has a specific purpose or end goal in mind for us, which we do not see or understand at the time.

The fact that God chooses someone for a specific purpose does not automatically imply willingness on that person's part. The fulfilment of God's purposes thus still has to happen without a violation of the laws of free will. So at the inception, when purpose is birthed in the heart, a clash of wills (God's will versus our will) is inevitable. This, I must add, is something that is not entirely foreign to God. God had to deal with this from Adam, who turned against Him; from Moses, who was not willing (at first) to go to Pharaoh; from Jonah, who actually refused to go to Nineveh; et al. We are not always keen on wanting to follow God's direction for our lives, because we feel entitled to our own plans. It is at this point, when there is friction between two opposing wills, that purpose seeks surrender. The statement from Mary, "Let it be according to Your Word," is actually one of surrender. I think it is important to understand that surrender does not imply agreement but rather compliance. In Matthew 21:28–32, this aspect of surrender is clearly illustrated in Jesus's parable. Apart from the theological application of the text, wherein Jesus conveys the parable of the two sons who are sent to work in their father's vineyard, there is great personal application in relation to the will. The one son agreed but never complied. The other son never agreed (it was against his will), but he nonetheless complied to do the will of his father. And in Jesus's assessment, the latter one did the will of the Father in heaven.

When we stumble upon God's choice for our lives and our purpose is birthed, it does not necessarily mean that we don't have other plans or alternates. In the garden of Gethsemane, Jesus chose to do the will of God (to go to the cross) whilst His own will (not wanting to go to the cross) was still very much alive. It is not always that a sense purpose makes us feel "alive" and gives us a spring in our step, causing us to rise early to greet the day. Sometimes it seeks surrender as we, like Moses, stutter through it. The principle of surrender dictates that we cannot demonstrate true acceptance of God's will and purpose for our lives unless our own will be present and alive, notwithstanding that it is often contrary to God's.

Purpose reveals motive

Seeing that we have been graced with the ability to set the course of our own lives, we instinctively think that we know and understand ourselves better than God does. The truth is, we don't naturally or intuitively entrust the course of our lives to God.

One of the greatest revelations, I believe, that Jesus brought to us is found in:

> John 10:10: "The thief comes not, but to steal and to kill, and to destroy. I have come that they might have life and that they might have it more abundantly."

This important passage of scripture reveals *motive*.

According to the *Collins Compact Dictionary,*[1] the word "motive" is the same as "motif". "Motif" is defined as: "1. A theme elaborated on in a piece of music or literature; 2. A recurring shape in a design."

From the definition, we can deduce that motif gives a theme and a shape to action. It becomes the distinctive mark that keeps appearing in the silhouette and design of our actions and choices. The seedbed for actions is found in motives. Motives elicit reason and embody actions.

Firstly, the quoted passage of scripture reveals satan's motive for his desired involvement in our lives: to kill, steal, and destroy. No matter how innocent and sweet satan's involvement in any matter may be, the end result is always death and destruction. That is the recurring silhouette and design in all that satan does.

The same passage also reveals God's motive for His desiring to be involved in our lives: to give us life and abundance. Life and abundance are the distinctive marks and major themes that recur in any work God does. As a result of this recurring theme, we may trust God's motive.

The importance of trusting God's motive is this: when He starts to align us to a certain task or destiny and begins the work of His purpose, we, at first, cannot see the theme of the design or pattern. At inception, the design or pattern looks foreign and out of kilter with our desired destiny. The pattern is difficult to see, never mind follow. It is at this seemingly fragmented stage of the birth of purpose that the trusting of God's motive becomes fundamental. This is a period that no one who is walking with God can bypass. Joseph, although his destiny was to become the prince of Egypt, experienced an initial set of events (which triggered the road to his destiny) that was almost contrary to the end result. Although betrayal was a major theme running through his life, he had to choose to trust God's motive for his life. He said the following to Potiphar's wife during her temptation: "How then can I do this great wickedness, and sin against God" (Genesis 39:9)?

By this time, it should have been easy for Joseph to distrust God's motive. He had been through an extremely rough season, and he could easily have thought, "So what is there to trust? How can I believe that better days will ever arrive?" But although the season was rough and nothing around him was self-explanatory, he maintained that God must have had a good motive behind all that unfolded.

Job knew something about trusting God's motive, even when he was distorted and broken. He declared, "Though God slay me, yet I will trust Him." We cheat ourselves out of greatness when we suspect God's motive and then opt out of the process of fulfilling His purpose for our lives. God's very best for us is intensely correlated to the purity of our motives towards Him. When all is said and done, we will know, through the often fragmented picture of establishing our purpose, that God only ever meant good towards us.

Purpose seeks reconciliation

At the start of every work that God initiates, a perceived abnormality becomes apparent, and that abnormality is really only in line with our perception of the world in which we live. Such a perceived abnormality comes about because God's ways are not our ways and His thoughts are higher than our thoughts. Not all things are understood when Divinity collides with our humanity. In fact, the convergence of Divinity and humanity becomes (most of the time) a place of contradiction. Moses the stutterer was charged with going to tell Pharaoh, "Let my people go." Gideon, the least in his tribe and family, was chosen to destroy the Midianites. David's youth was not supposed to be a match for Goliath's battlefield experience. King Jesus was born in a stable, as there was no place for Him at the inn. Paul, a former persecutor of Christians, became a pillar of the New Testament church. The list goes on. As we reflect on our own lives, we notice that something appears to be almost out of line, that there is a note out of tune, a step out of rhythm – and this makes the idea that we have been chosen for a specific purpose questionable. Some context about our make-up does not fit the job description. The past is either too dark or too painful. Our qualifications are not up to scratch. We cannot speak well, or the money we have is too little for us to realise the dream. There will, more often than not, be a context about us that does not fit the bill. And as much as the context around us builds into what we perceive ourselves as being, there remains a difference between who we truly are and the context around us. I suggest that God chooses the person rather than the context. He sees the person and not the context. God said of one of David's brothers when they had all lined up so that it could be determined which one of them would be anointed for the kingship, "Look not on his countenance, nor the height of his stature, because I have refused him … but the Lord look on the heart" (1 Samuel 16:7). His context (the build and the look) was right, but he was not the right person (i.e. he did not have the heart to be king).

I suggest that God would rather choose the
right person in the wrong context than the
wrong person in the right context.

Of Gideon, who was the least of both his tribe and his family,
it is said the angel greeted him this way: "The Lord is with
you, you mighty man of valour" (Judges 6:12). The context
(Gideon's lowly state in his tribe and family) was wrong, but
he was the right person because his heart was right. I suggest
that God would rather choose the right person in the wrong
context than the wrong person in the right context. And
that is the dilemma of being chosen: long after God (who
is the ultimate authority) has made His choice, the vessel
continues to struggle with his or her context. This is the
point and place where the vessel should start reconciling
him- or herself to the choice God has made for his or her life.

As you may know, reconciliation is an accounting term
indicating a balance between the two sides (debits and
credits). When the two sides do not balance, a reconciling
item is needed to bring things into balance. Parts of our lives
can never balance against the purpose God has chosen for
us. I propose to you that the reconciliation item is His favour
(grace), to which we have to continually reconcile ourselves.
(In Chapter 9 of this book, I elaborate on this reconciling
item – favour/grace.)

Purpose seeks singleness

The declaration "Let it be according to Your Word" is one laden with a purpose-driven directive. As we reconcile ourselves to the purpose given in our hearts, we progressively move closer to a point of singleness. Purpose by definition demands a singleness of heart. For as long as we have a variety of options on our side, we do not fully embrace the thing placed inside our hearts. The following verses (emphasis added) describe the singleness of Jesus's life:

- Luke 4:43: "I *must* preach the kingdom of God to other cities also for therefore I am sent."
- Luke 9:22: "The Son of Man *must* suffer many things and be rejected of the elders and chief priest and scribes and be slain and be raised the third day."
- Luke 22:37: "For l say unto you that this that is written *must* yet be accomplished in me."
- Luke 24:7: "Saying the Son of Man *must* be delivered into the hands of sinful men, and be crucified."
- John 3:14: "And as Moses lifted up the serpent in the wilderness even so *must* the Son of man be lifted up."
- John 9:4: "I *must* work the works of Him that sent me."
- John 12:23: "The Son of Man *must* be lifted up."
- John 20:9: "For as yet they knew not the scripture that he *must* raise again from the dead."

We see a golden thread, a singleness – namely, the word "must" – running through the life of Jesus. In light of our own lives, the "must" does not mean that we don't have options. On the contrary, it means that in the very midst of many options, one choice is elevated above the others. One particular thing supersedes the rest. That thing gets prioritised differently in the heart. Some things can be done and others may be done, but then there are the things that *must* be done. Some roads can be travelled and others may be travelled, but then there are those that *must* be travelled. That "must" is the inevitable something we have to go through, the situation we have to face, the decision we have to make, without which the sum of our lives would be infinitely less had we not engaged with that "must".

When Jesus came to Gethsemane, He had an option, His will, but He also knew there was a "must", the Father's will. He surrendered His will and reconciled Himself to the singleness of the Father's will when He said, "Not My will, but Yours be done." The life of Paul, like the lives of all great people, had the same trademark:

- Acts 9:6: "Arise, and go into the city and it shall be told thee what thou *must* do."
- Acts 9:16: "For l will show him how great things he *must* suffer for my Name's sake."

Unless we reconcile ourselves to the singleness that is required, we can never be successful at living or at fulfilling our purpose. Purpose is only at home in a resolved person.

Purpose gives power

Reconciling ourselves to a singleness of purpose is essential for retaining our focus. It becomes an issue of being purpose-driven over desire-driven. We have been graced with the exceptional blessing to choose, i.e. the power of choice.

That in itself means we have been blessed with power. This "power blessing", the ability to choose, gives humankind a unique ability over the rest of creation in two respects: firstly, the ability to give ourselves to something. Every one of us gives ourselves to something, whether we are conscious of it or not. Whilst the power to choose is very satisfying and liberating, the result of our choices is not always as satisfying and liberating. When we choose to give ourselves to something, we give, through the legitimate power of choice, ownership of ourselves to such an entity.

Hence the very strange phenomenon of inanimate things, e.g. money, alcohol, and other drugs, "owning" people. By the same token, we take on the nature of whatever we choose to give ourselves to.

The "power blessing", the ability to choose, gives humankind a unique ability over the rest of creation – the ability to give ourselves to something.

The second ability that the blessing of choice brings with it is the ability to become. The more we choose to respond in a certain way, the more we become what we respond to. And whilst we are celebrating and exercising this glorious gift of choice, we cannot help but ask why more people in the world today, are tired, are lethargic, and have very little sense of direction in our life. Why is it that our choices are weakening us instead of strengthening us? I believe the key is this: not everything we give ourselves to gives back to us. And that is a key feature of purpose: it gives as much back to us as we give to it, which brings about a balance to the flow of energy. Purpose is the adrenalin of the inner person. Power and passion are derived from purpose. After Jesus had reconciled Himself to the will of the Father, the scripture says, "And there appeared an angel unto Him from heaven, strengthening Him" (Luke 22:43). This is a clear illustration that the power flow from purpose is always vertical. God, being the giver of purpose, will always fuel us with power and passion when we choose His choice. When we choose to give ourselves vertically, i.e. to God's idea for our lives, the power supply for our lives comes from above. By the same the token, if we choose to give ourselves *only* horizontally, to people and/or to our own plans and ideas, the powers supply comes only from ourselves, which is not sustainable. The energy drainage and emptiness starts when we continually give horizontally what we have not received vertically. We can only serve our fellows effectively by drawing on what we receive from above.

The road to understanding our purpose starts when we declare from our heart, "Let it be according to Your Word."

"Let it be to me according to Your Word" (Luke 1:38).

Summary of Chapter 4

1. Purpose is birthed in us by our coming into contact with God's choice for our life.

2. True surrender to God's will and purpose cannot be demonstrated unless our own will is present.

3. God would rather choose the right person in the wrong context than the wrong person in the right context.

4. Purpose seeks singleness of heart.

5. The energy drainage and emptiness starts when we continually give horizontally what we have not received vertically.

6. Purpose gives power.

7. What we must do is not always comfortable.

8. The power blessing, the ability to choose, gives humankind a unique ability over the rest of creation: the ability to give ourselves to something.

CHAPTER 5

IF I AM FAVOURED, WHY ARE PEOPLE DESERTING ME?

Let it be unto me according to Your Word.

Luke 1:38

When a sheep sees a flock of sheep, he sees security. A goat, however, may see an opportunity to take control. When sheep see a shepherd, they see leadership, but when a goat sees a shepherd, he may see a challenge to his own authority.

Perry Stone

Imbued with a sense of purpose, Joseph feels that he is part of something bigger than himself. The reality of the dream in which the angel appeared to him has taken root in his heart. The path to where all this is leading is not clear, but Joseph has found a willingness in his heart to follow it. He can hardly believe he was going to walk out on Mary on the basis of his ignorance. Mary's being chosen has drawn him into something he had heard spoken of by prophets and in the synagogue. As a result of his relationship with Mary, he finds himself in the heart of something divine that will change the course of his life as well as the course of history. He was not present when Mary declared, "Let it be according to Your Word," but as a result of his being part of her life, he is tasked to stay with her. It is unfathomable to him that God has visited his doorstep. That the culmination of years of prophetic utterances will find fulfilment through his house is unbelievable to Joseph.

There is a tangible build-up in the expectation of the coming Messiah. In town, reports are making the rounds that the birth of the Messiah is imminent, according to the foresight given by the prophets. Joseph and Mary are not sure if they should speak up and confirm the rumours. They have shared the celestial news with a few close friends, but they quickly realised that not everyone shares their excitement. In fact, a few people close to them have become distant in their scepticism. From the response of others with whom he and Mary have shared the news, Joseph gets a glimpse of himself when he was on the same side of the cynicism fence. He understands that some people battle with believing the news and that others simply outright reject the notion of Mary's having been chosen to be the mother of the Messiah. Joseph understands from his own experience as an ex-sceptic the amount of patience that will be required when dealing with the people surrounding him and Mary. Their varied responses, he believes, are not personally directed at him and Mary. But rather, consciously or unconsciously, their respective responses is a reflection of their view to God's having chosen them for the purpose of conceiving the Messiah. Some are happy; others are envious; and still others remain unconvinced. Joseph realises his naivety in thinking that all of them would respond the same. A spectrum of vantage points has become apparent from all of the people with whom they have shared the news. He is realising that trying to convince people that he and Mary have been chosen is fruitless, energy-sapping, focus-bending and completely counterproductive. Joseph decides to disengage from the debates with people about what he knows he has heard. He, like Mary before him, cannot prove anything, but he simply has to continue walking according to what he knows. The path has been carved for him.

As the good carpenter that he is, Joseph understands building processes – but in this process, he cannot quite see how everything will hinge together. He did not choose himself; neither did Mary choose herself. The choice was made for them. Joseph discerns a change in direction of their lives as a result of their having been chosen, a shift that feels natural in its course. It feels both exiting and uncertain – exciting because of the divine flavour to it, and uncertain because all of the details have yet to unfold. The reactions of people to the news that they have been chosen is beyond their control. They have agreed to God's choice. They have to live with it, and so do others. Their path has been set. God has chosen.

* * *

It is absolutely intriguing to observe people's reactions when they watch an intense drama or a soap opera. They become unyieldingly gripped and immensely involved in the story and in the interpretation of the storylines of the respective characters. And sometimes, if not all the time, it is the mixture of frustration, suspense, and satisfaction from the story that keeps viewers glued to the story. They experience suspense from wanting to see how a certain event or storyline will unfold; frustration when the unfolding deviates from their expectations; and satisfaction when the story does unfold in line with their expectations. All the commotion and wishing from the viewers does not help them to (always) get the outcome they want, because the outworking of the story is true only to the script. The story will unfold and end as it was written. The role players in the story are merely being faithful to act out what has been written, i.e. the script.

I believe that this analogy bears relevance to the discussion of being chosen and favoured. Should we make this analogy applicable to the story of life, the cast for the division of roles would look something this:

1. Author (Scriptwriter): God

2. Main actor/actress: You and I (in our own lives)

3. Supporting actors/actresses: The people close to us

4. Guest actors/actresses: The people playing a temporary role in our lives

5. Viewers: The people at the sidelines of our lives

Why is it important to understand the role division of life in a discussion concerning having God's favour, being chosen, and having been assigned a purpose? I believe that the short answer to this question is that both the necessary motivation and or distraction for the task at hand will come through people. If we don't have an understanding of the role division, then we will never adequately focus on the task at hand.

1. The Author: God

To believe in God is to believe that we are here by design and not by default, as I have stated in the Preface. It means that God, as the giver and initiator of life, is a purposeful God and the ultimate giver of purpose. From this premise, we deduce that no one is born without a purpose, i.e. a script. Truth be told, it is sometimes very difficult to follow the script in the midst of the often monotonous rhythm of day-to-day living.

As the Author of life, God has not "programmed" us according to each day. The complication of such a view would be the place of free will and choice, which are fundamental to being "created in His image and likeness". Without the concept of free will, humanity cannot be considered to have been made in the image and likeness of God. So how do we reconcile God as the Author of life and our being gifted free will?

Firstly, I suggest that a fundamental part of the idea of life is embedded in the concept of partaking. To partake means to give oneself to something already given. In the equation of partaking, one part thereof is not from us – namely, life. God is the giver and the Creator of life. Secondly, it would appear that God has set the functioning of free will within the boundaries of two particular core aspects (as discussed below) in relation to Himself. I believe that we witness this setting from the inception in the Garden of Eden, when God set the boundary – "You shall not eat of it [the tree of knowledge of good and evil]" (Genesis 2:17) – but inside that boundary Adam and his wife were to "freely eat" (Genesis 2:16). Within the perimeter of the limitation, there was enough room for Adam and Eve to express free will. Similarly, we can partake freely of the options available in life. We can decide to marry or to remain single; to have children or not; to study any discipline and practise any profession we wish; and so forth. In short, we can choose. God never intended to run our day, but He does want to – as He did in the Garden of Eden, where Adam could freely eat – have fellowship with us. I want us to consider that as the Author of life, God has set the perimeter of the limitation of our free will around two core aspects, as follows:

Whatever we do should bring glory to God

Though fundamentally we are at liberty to do and to choose, when we do so it should bring glory to God. Glorifying God is a response we give to that part of the "partaking" equation which we did not provide – life. We found life here not because we created it ourselves, but because God, the Creator of life, allowed us to partake of it. So the perimeter is set for glorifying God.

We should function within the confines of our giftings and talents

I believe that the birth of Jesus is illustrative of what happens when we are born into this life. On the evening when Jesus was born, He received gold, frankincense, and myrrh. This, I suggest, is a symbolic indication of the setting of life, the setting of the script. Our experience of the gift of life is a blending of gold, frankincense, and myrrh. Gold typifies the giftings and talents that we were born with, those things which enable us to function and to respond positively to the gift of life. Frankincense typifies our worship of God. Myrrh is demonstrative of the often bitter taste to life, of its challenges and vicissitudes, which none of us can escape. In isolation, our talents would produce pride, and in seclusion the bitter taste to life would leave us hopeless. But our worship of God serves as a blender for our talents and our challenges, to produce a savoury taste to life. Against this scenery has the Author of life written the setting of life. It is within the confines of this scenery that we have to live out our purpose and choosing.

Our worship of God serves as a blender for
our talents and our challenges, to produce a
savoury taste to life.

---

2. Main actor/actress

To further the concept of partaking, I propose that we are not born into this life by right but by privilege. Through being born into this life, we were granted the allowance to partake of life. Life is beautiful.

The writer of Psalm 139:13, 15 conveys the following: "Thou hast *covered* me in my mother's womb … when I was *made* in secret."

After reading these two verses, we can deduce that you and I were made before we were conceived in the womb. No person has ever made another. When we have children of our own, we merely conceive (in the womb) what was made in secret. God made you and me in secret, wrote the script for our lives, and covered us in our mothers' wombs to be born into this world.

As main actors and actresses of our own lives, we have the responsibility to partake of what was given. On this basis, we cannot think up a purpose and then give ourselves to it. Should we do this, then we are no longer partaking, as we are both giving the purpose and giving ourselves to it- remember one part of the equation of partaking should not come from us. Adam and Eve did not make any of the trees in the Garden of Eden. All of them were given. Adam and Eve partook through giving themselves. When Jesus Christ stood before the challenge of the cross, He allowed His disciples to partake of His body and His blood. Jesus further expanded on this concept when He said, "unless you eat the flesh of the Son of Man and drink His blood, you have no life in you (John 6: 53)." The message is clear: we have a responsibility to partake of what was given. This requires that we be present in our own lives in order to fulfil the acting role subscribed to us. Being absent from one's own life is one of the greatest injustices that a person can inflict on him- or herself. Satisfaction can only be experienced within the confines of our own script by our being present throughout the frustrations and suspense in order to maximise the fulfilment.

The earthly life of Jesus is an example of how we should order our own lives. One of the most profound verses of scripture pertaining to the life of Jesus is found in Matthew 26:24: "The Son of Man goes only as it is written of him."

Josh McDowell writes the following in *The Best Josh McDowell: A Ready Defense*[1]:

> In the Old Testament there are sixty major messianic prophesies and approximately 270 ramifications fulfilled in one person, Jesus Christ. It is helpful to look at these predictions fulfilled in Christ as His "address." You have probably never realised how important your name and address are – and yet these details set you apart from five billion other people who also inhabit the planet. ... The specifics of this [Jesus's] address can be found in the Old Testament, a document written over a period of thousand years, which contains more than three hundred references to His coming.

These are staggering facts, ones that communicate to us that long before Jesus was conceived and born, the script of His life was written and settled. I don't believe, from a "planning our purpose" point of view, that God would deal any differently with you and me. As alluded to before, one part of the equation of partaking should not come from us. Instead, playing the main role in our own life means that we have a responsibility to give ourselves to our given purpose.

An important point to realise in relation to our being the main actor or actress in our own life is the following: seeing that God, the giver of purpose, has provided the setting of life and the limits for our expression of free will, He is qualified to be our judge. This implies that although I have a right to anything, I don't necessarily have entitlement to everything, just as Adam had a right to anything in the garden but had no entitlement to partake of a certain tree. It would be extremely arrogant of us to think we can live in any which way we want. It would thus make sense, and be worthwhile, to give ourselves unto the script the Author has written for us. I give back to the Author when I yield myself to the role He has chosen for me to play.

To partake means to give oneself to something already given.

---

3. Supporting actors/actresses

Supporting actors/actresses are generally the people who are close to us, those with a sense of permanency in our lives. Inasmuch as we are the main actors/actresses in our own lives, we are also compelled to play a supporting role in the lives of other people. The role we have to fulfil is never isolated. God has an integrated master plan, part of His bigger purpose. His plans and purposes are cohesive and inclusive; hence, the chosen vessel(s) can never be isolated. Depending on the circumstances, we switch roles between being the main character and the supporting actor/actress. Thus, we get the divine opportunity to partake in helping others accomplish either parts of their script or their entire script. The blessing in supporting others lies in the opportunity afforded to us to partake in the favour bestowed on their lives. The shared favour from their lives becomes key in helping us to complete our own script. When we respond in the correct way, through support, to the purpose of God for others, we develop humility and increase our own potential for fulfilling our own script. If all we do is play the main role, then we dispose ourselves to becoming self-centred. We ought to support as much as we take the main stage.

The entire idea of supporting others in their assignment is also embedded in the concept of partaking. When we support, we are not merely helping; we are partaking. Our willingness, or lack thereof, to support others is a clear indication of our response to God's choices and purpose. In fact, it is indicative of the level of humility in our hearts. It answers the question of whether or not we understand that our lives and assignments are a part of God's bigger purpose.

The brothers of Joseph are a case in point. They responded to Joseph in an antagonistic way after he had communicated to them God's purpose for his life, the part he had received. Joseph did not create or think up that part. It was that part (not given by Joseph, but given to him) to which his brothers responded with hatred and hostility. Joseph did not choose himself, but he was chosen. The vessel was hated over the Maker's choice, which is part of the dilemma of being chosen. David's brothers were no different. Their view of him changed, possibly, on the day he was anointed and became "chosen over them".

Our willingness to support others in their quest is, in fact, a response to the One who did the choosing. Hence, we cannot base the legitimacy of our assignment on the level of support we receive. Often, we simply have to continue walking in what we believe we should do.

4. Guest actors/actresses

Guest actors/actresses are those people who come and go as we travel through life. They have a temporary role for a specific season and seldom go through all the way with us. And I think the key here is that these people play a temporary role with a specific purpose. They are, as the word denotes, guests in our lives. It is important to realise that in the same way that other people enter my life and serve a temporary and specific purpose, I may be a "guest" in another's life. Guests play a critical linkage role when we are near the horizon of a significant part of the fulfilment of our purpose. I believe that the linkage role is prescribed to the guest because by the time we edge closer to destiny and breakthrough our support is almost always out of reach or has started to tire.

The butler in the case of Joseph took on the role of guest. By the time Joseph met the butler, the former was close to being completely exhausted. The journey had been long and hurtful, with an end not yet in sight. The butler was not with Joseph from the beginning, but he appeared in his life towards the end of Joseph's tests, near the cusp of his breakthrough. The butler was there to provide a linkage to the completion (from a preparatory point of view) of Joseph's script. By the time the butler arrived, Joseph had zero support around him. The butler appeared and then disappeared, only to reappear later to tell Pharaoh about Joseph.

When Jesus was led away to be crucified and His cross became heavy, Simon, a Cyrenian, was compelled to bear His cross for Him (Luke 23:26). The miracles, including the feeding of the multitudes, were great, but the cross was about purpose. During the miracles, Jesus had the support of His disciples to manage the crowds and so forth. But when He came to the gate of His purpose, He had no support; there were no disciples to help Him. It took the appearance of a "guest", Simon, to carry His cross for a moment. The criticality of those few minutes and those few metres for which Simon carried His cross is something we will never be able to comprehend.

On the cross, Jesus had to battle to stay alive until a certain time, 3 p.m. – to cover the evening sacrifice. He could not die prematurely. In the greater scheme of things, the "small" linkage that Simon provided was, in fact, beyond significant. The contribution from Simon was immeasurable in the end. The few minutes for which Simon carried the cross were a few minutes added to Jesus's strength so He could fully accomplish the work of redemption. The few steps that Simon offered in support were a few steps added to Jesus's reach to pave the way to salvation for humankind.

In order to step into fulfilling our purpose, sometimes after painful battles, each one of us is in need of a guest to provide the final linkage. Guests usually appear at the threshold of destiny's door, when we are in need of that final push to reach for the door. But whilst we are awaiting a guest, let us not fail to be the guest in someone else's life.

5. Viewers

The viewers are those people who are at the sidelines of our lives. Observers with little or no influence, they, as I mentioned when providing the analogy of soap operas, would wish for the storyline to be parallel to their desire for it. Is it not ironic how we, sometimes illogically, accommodate the viewers at the expense of the supporters, how we consider the viewers' feelings and opinions when our script goes contrary to popular opinion? When decisions become controversial, the subtle pressure to change them normally comes from the viewers. May I remind you that the viewers only seek entertainment, will always criticise, and will become frustrated when you do not do what they think you should do? Viewers are there only to *wish* our lives would shape up according to their preference.

The apostle Paul wrote the following liberating thought in Romans 14:4: "Who are you to judge another's servant. To his own master he stands of falls. …" The servant stands or falls by his Lord, by his Master. The viewers may have the liberty to judge and criticise all they want, but in the end the actor/actress remains accountable to satisfy the pen of the Scriptwriter. The One who wrote the script, who gave the purpose, is superior to the viewers. By Him, not by the opinion of the viewer, do we stand or fall. When all is said and done, we are here to fulfil the divine purpose of the Creator. Yes, we do have a Master, a Scriptwriter who is eligible to be our judge. We all stand or fall by Him. We often model our lives around the question that God will possibly ask us one day: "What have you done with your life?" But what if, just maybe, the question actually turns out to be, "Have you done with your life what I [the Lord] has purposed for it?" I think the second question is completely different in its directive from the first one. The first question almost implies that I can do with my life as I please – and technically, through free will and choice, I can – but it neglects the idea that I do not stand or fall by myself. The second question has a purpose-directive to it. It carries the idea of the One by whom I stand or fall, which is in no way foreign to what Jesus declared: "Father I have glorified you in the earth and have finished the work you gave me to do" (John 17:4).

In this verse, Jesus summarises both the setting of life (as alluded earlier) and the perimeter of free will: we are here to glorify God on the earth and to finish the work He has given to us. I believe that these two aspects became the "law" whereby Jesus conducted His entire earthly life. Therefore, we should follow suit. Jesus mixed and mingled with all types of people, to the point where the religious sects of His day accused Him of being a sinner, a drunkard, a demon-possessed man, etc. He conversed with a Samaritan woman at a well, something forbidden in His day. He was criticised for performing miracles on the Sabbath. His detractors grew, and they called Him names, but Jesus knew who these people were: viewers. He understood that His Father was incomparably more superior to those viewers.

Unless we frame our earthly life around glorifying God and doing the work of the Father given to us, we will not be successful in separating the viewers from the supporters. It is draining when we attempt to gear all our efforts towards not wanting to be misunderstood once we embark upon the purpose He has placed inside us. We have to live "disconnected" from the viewers if we want to give our purpose a chance at fulfilment. We owe it to ourselves to focus our attention and energy on the fact of our having been chosen for whatever task. God's assignment favours us, and His favour assigns us. Within the confines of our script, we have His favour, which enables us to act out on life's stage the role assigned to us.

"Let it be unto me according to Your Word" (Luke 1:38).

Summary of Chapter 5

1. We can divide the roles for life's script as follows:

    o   Author (Scriptwriter): God
    o   Main actor/actress: You and I (in our own lives)
    o   Supporting actors/actresses: The people close to us
    o   Guest actors/actresses: The people who play a temporary role in our lives
    o   Viewers: The people at the sidelines of our lives

2. Our worship of God serves as a blender, producing a savoury taste to life.

3. Through being born into this life, we were granted the allowance to partake of life.

4. The idea of partaking conveys that something has been given, something to which I am called to give myself.

CHAPTER 6

IF I AM FAVOURED, WHY DOES IT FEEL AS IF MY LIFE IS GOING IN CIRCLES?

Let it be unto me according to Your Word.

Luke 1:38

Hours with God make minutes with men effective.

Dr Myles Munroe

It is with nervousness and anxiety that Mary remembers her only response, "Let it be according to Your Word," as labour pangs sweep through her body. Amidst her contractions, she has strong flashbacks of that day. The appearance of the angel is still as vivid in Mary's mind as it was on the very day it happened. The memory of the atmosphere, the holiness, is almost tangible. The vibrations of the awe-inspiring words remain inside her as she reflects on the event through her mind's eye. Before the divine encounter, Mary found life to be neither exciting nor boring. Life was plateaued on normality. She had always been just a normal girl in relation to any other young girl. Nothing about her suggested that she was "special" or "chosen". In fact, everything and everyone around her seemed wrapped in the ordinary and in commonness, to the extent that nurturing anything outside the status quo is disallowed.

Since the first kick of her baby, Mary has been occupied with the functional evolution of her life. She is going to be a first-time mother, having carried and nurtured the Saviour of the world for a full nine months. It has been an intense nine months, wherein she has exhausted the emotional spectrum, including her joyful ecstasy when the angel appeared to her and her months of uncertainty about Joseph's reaction. But as the intensity of the moment reaches its peak, Mary, though embattled with excruciating pain, finds herself questioning the absolute normality of the process. "The announcement of His birth was marked by angelic visitations and divine power. Shouldn't His birth be less painful and less normal?" she argues in her feeble mind as she ebbs and flows through the pain pendulum. Joseph has been from the one inn to the next, seeking to secure a place fit for the birth of the King, but he has had no success. Completely baffled by Divinity's dependence on humanity, Joseph, totally out of options, is forced to settle for a lowly stable.

Mary battles through the burden of the moment. She comes close to losing consciousness as strength and blood flow from her body. She faintly hears Joseph's supportive voice as he begs for a final push. With every ounce of strength she has left in her, Mary gives one final push and then gives birth to the Saviour of the world. Moments later, the couple hear angelic choirs ushering in His arrival. Celebrated by cosmic joy and welcomed by the animal kingdom, the newborn baby is held and caressed by Mary and Joseph.

It is the King in the frail body of a baby. Mary and Joseph are completely overwhelmed by the sense of collaboration between Divinity and humanity. They are covered in blissful joy as rivers of delight and peace flush away the anxiety and pain of the birthing process. The arrival of the King has for now silenced their wondering about the not so hassle-free process and the unavailability of the best places for His birth. The stable full of animals does not matter anymore, as the Creator has come to creation. Mary, now that she has given birth to the King, feels that she has accomplished a big part of her mission, for the time being at least.

* * *

When we are chosen for a particular assignment, we have an unspoken expectation that things should just happen and fall into place for us. Whilst eventually things do fall into place, there is an interim when they don't. It is during this point of the process that we feel we sometimes have to do more than God is doing. It really becomes an issue of roles and responsibilities between us and God. When we do find ourselves in those perceived bad and stubborn situations, the lines between humanity's responsibility and Divinity's responsibility tend to become blurred to us. It is less difficult to think of oneself as favoured after the breakthrough, when basking in the sunshine after the storm and when the waters for sailing are calm. But it is during the in-between time when uncertainty grips our heart and attacks our mind. On a creation level, we know we are blessed because we are created in God's image and likeness, but the translation thereof into a functional level appears to be difficult to explain or digest. The process of reconciling our being favoured and chosen on both the creation level and the functional level proves challenging, creating a potential breeding ground for doubt and spiritual fatigue. I believe, though, that we can put together a picture of the process or cycle, from the inception of our choosing to the fulfilment of our purpose, by tracing the architecture of God's hand as reflected in several people in the Bible. I think an understanding of the process, although not always generic, does give some sense of direction when we do find it hard to locate ourselves on the radar screen of the process.

Although we are chosen divinely, for whatever task, we still have to give birth to our calling- in a humanly manner.

The mixture of emotions and expectations, sometimes illogical, it must be said, can create so much confusion that we might seriously consider aborting our mission. A key facet of our misperception is normally embedded in our understanding of the collaboration between Divinity and humanity. Our expectation is that because God has birthed purpose in our heart, that purpose will be established in a divine manner. Yet although we are chosen divinely, for whatever task, we still have to give birth to our calling – in a humanly manner in most cases. It is with the almost normality of the divine process that we sometimes battle. But I believe that our reflecting on understanding the cycle will produce in us courage and illumination to continue on our walk towards what was birthed in our hearts. In addition to discussing some biblical characters, I suggest six generic phases to the process of our choosing and purpose.

1. Discovery phase

Objective of this phase: To produce in us singleness of pursuit

Everything we want to do or be starts with a discovery. To discover something means to uncover what has been hidden. To discover, in the context of being chosen for a particular assignment or purpose, does not mean to go on a treasure hunt but rather to stumble upon and then grow into an understanding of one's assignment. The discovery phase is really a peeling phase or an unwrapping process, if you will. The God who hid purpose in our hearts is the only One who can do the unwrapping thereof without damaging the contents. The apostle Paul, in Galatians 1:15–16, conveys four fundamental principles pertaining to the discovery phase of being chosen:

"But when it pleased God, who separated me from my mother's womb, and called me by his grace. To reveal His Son in me."

1. Time – "When it pleased God"

Both the discovery and the evolution of any functional assignment is dependent on the kairological (divine timing and unfolding of events) allowance from God. God's timing is His prerogative. God is functional on the earth and in the affairs of people. He both allows and orchestrates certain events to bring us closer to discovering what He has placed in our hearts. Moses, for example, did not go look for God in the desert; he almost accidently (from a human perspective) walked into the burning bush. As a consequence, his choosing was as a result of God being pleased. Joseph's conveyance of his dreams got him sold and also linked him to a discovery of his assignment because it pleased God. The same process in our own lives will happen no differently.

2. Separation "Who separated me"

In using the natural analogy of being separated from his mother's womb, Paul establishes a spiritual principle which simply means that we cannot evolve functionally unless we are separated from that which is familiar. In the natural world, a person cannot grow to become a young boy or girl, have a career, become a father or mother, and so forth unless he or she leaves his or her mother's womb. The concept of separation ultimately entails that we leave behind things (in some cases people) not compatible to the advancement of God's choice for us. Truthfully, such separation is almost always a painful process. It can be extremely unsettling, psychologically draining, and emotionally taxing. Naturally speaking, it is this separation process from the mother that causes babies to cry at birth as they enter a new environment away from the mother's womb. It is said, unless the baby is touched and comforted within a reasonable time frame after birth, permanent psychological and emotional problems could be embedded in the baby's psychological make-up. In a spiritual context, such a separation process can take on many forms, but the fundamental thrust of the phase is to produce singleness of focus, knowing that the touch and hand of God will never leave us.

No calling will ever be treated with reverence
and priority unless the Caller is reverenced.

It is only by being separated from whatever could possibly hinder the advancement of our choosing and purpose that we will set our attention and affection on our purpose.

3. Calling – "Who called me"

There are two parts to every separation process: a separation from and then an attachment to. We are not leaving something without cleaving to something else. There is no calling without a caller, no assignment without an assignor, and no choice without a chooser. The separation process sets us up for attachment to the One "who called *us*" (italics added). No calling will ever be treated with reverence and priority unless the Caller is reverenced. It is from this premise that humility is birthed in the human heart. It would be senseless to know of the vision or assignment without knowing or having a relationship with the giver thereof. The depth of our response to whatever calling or purpose is indicative of our reverence of the One who called us.

4. Revelation – "Reveal His Son in me"

This is the single purpose at the heart of any and every assignment from God: to reveal Christ in us. John wrote of Christ, "All things were made by Him and without Him was not anything made that was made" (John 1:3). Everything that was created, be it purpose, calling, or ministry, has been created by Him, through Him, and for Him. Thus, the revelation of anything we are called to do is dependent on the revelation of Christ in us. Everything is encapsulated in Him. I believe that we sometimes err in concentrating more on what can be revealed through us rather than on what can be revealed in us: "Christ in you [me] the hope of glory" (Colossians 1:27). Unless we have a strong sense of what is being revealed in us, we cannot truly understand the purpose of what will be revealed through us. The word "reveal" implicitly assumes that something is present and is only to be illuminated. Christ is in me, but He has to be revealed to me.

When we create outside of us what has not been created in us, our own creation tends to destroy us in the end.

This appears to be the way that God chooses to operate. He has hidden inside us everything that we need in order to become what we ought to be. I believe that some of our struggles start when we want to create something for ourselves outside of what has been created in us. When we create outside of us what has *not* been created in us, our own creation tends to destroy us in the end. But when we build on what has been created in us, it normally establishes us. In short, it is fruitless deviating from the purpose placed in our heart. I believe that the discovery phase should not be as mystical as it is sometimes made out to be. Seeing that God is the One who places purpose and calling in our heart, who other than God can reveal it to us? We are thus inevitably called to walk closer to the Lord.

I think it is safe to liken the discovery phase to the use of appliances and electrical current in our homes. The electrical current cannot be seen with the naked eye, but it is still there. The appliances, if not plugged in, cannot serve their purpose. But once plugged in, each appliance functions in accordance with its design and intent. This simple analogy illustrates the fact that although design and intent, according to our purpose, have been placed inside us, connecting to the current (Christ in us) will cause us to function in accordance to what has been created inside of us.

2. Decision phase

Objective of this phase: To hand God legal authority to activate what He has placed inside us

Although an angel appeared to Mary to tell her that she was highly favoured for the purpose of giving birth to the Saviour, she still had to respond to that call. And so do we have to respond to what we are called to do. The decision phase encapsulates our response to that which has been placed inside us. Just as Mary responded, "Let it be according to Your Word," so Jesus responded, "Not my will but Yours be done." Through our response, we either allow or disallow God legal authority to activate His choice for our lives. It is the simple act of a decision that activates God's choice over us. In the previous chapter, we elaborated on the concept of partaking, where at least one side of the equation should not come from us. The decision phase is the other side of the equation, indicating where our decision either activates or leaves dormant God's chosen purpose for our life. This is in line with the Divinity–humanity collaboration.

Why are decisions so important? The expression of free will, which is a critical function of being made in the image and likeness of God, is obviously dependent on our decision-making ability. Decisions are the doorway to possible paths and the seed that links us to specific paths. If we think about Adam in the Garden of Eden, we see that the tree of knowledge of good and evil was dormant until the seed of a decision from Adam and Eve activated its fruit so it could become legally operable in humankind. Adam and Eve did not die immediately from eating the fruit, but the seed of decision activated death to legally take its course throughout the ages. The inverse, based on the same principle, took place when Jesus was faced with the prospect of the cross in the garden of Gethsemane. It was only when He said, "Not My will but Yours be done," that angels came to strengthen Him. The decision, the yes, activated the power and grace of God. It also gave God legal authority to activate His saving grace for humankind. The seed of that decision brought us into the kingdom of God many, many years after the decision had been made. On the basis of the seed of that decision, the power of Jesus's blood to cleanse people of sin still has, and always will have, legal authority on the earth.

> When we reject God's choice for our lives, we
> are not rejecting God, but we are in essence
> rejecting ourselves, who we are, what we should
> do, our identity, and what we can become.

At one stage, God was so frustrated with the Israelites that He told them, "I put before you life and death ... choose life" (Deuteronomy 30:19). The message is clear: through the seed of decision we can activate either life or death. The conception to life of any creature happens when an egg and a sperm come together. If you will, the calling, for whatever purpose, has been placed inside of us only as potential (the egg). When we respond positively to such potential by declaring, "Let it be unto me according to Your Word," our decision acts as "a sperm" to activate that potential. At the time of having to sow the seed of decision, we normally find ourselves caught up in other options. But history and reality have always shown the will of God to be the better choice amongst our possible options. And the vital thing about God's will for our lives is this: God's will is His choice. When we reject God's choice for our lives, we are not rejecting God, but we are in essence rejecting ourselves, who we are, what we should do, our identity, and what we can become. We are in fact rejecting our future. On the other hand, when we decide to commit our lives to the Lord, we may not see a difference immediately (although sometimes we do), but our end will never be as our beginning, as the seed of our decision gives the Lord legal authority to go at work with what He has placed in us.

3. Developmental phase

Objective of this phase: To align our energy and focus to the nature of the One calling us

Through observation, it would appear that there is a generic core of pressure points against which we have to develop. The sphere of our development seldom goes outside the sphere of the following pressure points:

o   Faithfulness
    Faithfulness measures how much we value and understand what we have. Esau, for example, did not think much of his birth right, so he sold it to his brother, a clear sign of how much he thought of it.

o   Money
    Money, whether we lack it or have it in abundance, measures how we relate to power.

o   Perceived failure or success
    Our failure or our success gauges our emotional loyalty. When terror struck in the lives of Job and his wife, Job's wife could not wait to walk out on God and her husband.

o   Faith
    Genuine faith is a sign of humility. Having faith is an indication that we trust the One who is bigger than we are.

o Loss

Loss brings us closer to the question of ownership: do we understand to whom we belong? It is impossible to go through life without experiencing losses. Whether it is the loss of employment, material things, or a loved one, we will face losses in this life sooner or later.

o Self-control

Our self-control measures our willingness to trust. When we are being tested, our level of patience and endurance is an indication of our level of self-control.

o Forgiveness

Forgiveness shows our understanding of love. We forgive as much as we know we are loved.

Why is it important for us to be put through some form of development? I believe that a big part of our development is linked to aligning us to the nature of He who has chosen us. Inasmuch as being chosen brings honour to the vessel, the vessel should also bring honour to the One who made the choice. Somehow the gap in nature between the One who made the choice and the vessel needs to be closed. This usually happens during the developmental phase.

I can't have the ability to become but not given
the free will to choose just as I can't have the
free will to choose but not be given the
ability to become.

It is through being developed that we are moulded and shaped. In an earlier chapter, I described humans as image-beings. As image-beings, we have been given both the ability to become and the gift of independent free will. I can't have the ability to become but not be given the free will to choose just as I can't have the free will to choose but not be given the ability to become. If, for an example, I am given the ability to choose but not the ability to become, then my ability to choose is powerless, as it has no effect on the shaping of my life. For the power of choice to be effective, we must have the accompanying ability to become (i.e. to be moulded). During the decision phase, as explained before, we exercise the seed of choice, whereas in the development phase we demonstrate our ability to become through such choices. I believe that these abilities (to choose and become) form the basis for God's not giving up on us during the developmental phase. The Potter knows that the clay can be moulded.

The truth is that, such a moulding phase can sometimes feel extremely taxing, like there is no end to it. From time to time, we want to jump off the Potter's wheel. Sometimes we do jump off. But because we said yes, He picks us up again, in many cases for the umpteenth time, and resumes the moulding. Hebrews 12:2–7 gives us a clue about the emotional spectrum experienced during the developmental phase. We can do one of the following three things:

o   Despise the process
    This happens when we do not understand the Lord's objective for instigating certain processes in our life.

o   Faint
    It is important to note that the text does not read, "Die." When we faint, it means that our spiritual senses could not perceive properly. We normally faint when we feel overwhelmed by the developmental process. According to Hebrews 12:2, the actual reason for our fainting is the contradiction we suffer: what we feel and suffer versus our knowledge of God's nature will not match at the time.

o   Endure
    When we are being moulded, we are called to endure. Our Lord Jesus, according to the text, endured the cross and despised the contradiction of the cross. Our development, irrespective of the degree of difficulty, always takes place "according to the integrity of His heart and the skilfulness of His hands" (Psalm 78:72).

4. Disillusionment phase

Objective of this phase: To bring us to the realisation that we are chosen based on His strength

The disillusionment phase deals with the "how" part of our assignment. We have numerous examples of people throughout scripture who were disillusioned when they realised the size of the task to which God was calling them. Moses was so disillusioned when he heard that he had to go to Pharaoh that he asked, "Who am I" (Exodus 3:11)? He felt very small in relation to the might of Pharaoh. Abraham too reached such a stage. The size of what God had promised him and his human inability to bring it to fruition produced such frustration that he tried to do it in his own strength. The fruit of his frustration led to the birth of Ishmael (more frustration). When Gideon came into contact with his assignment, he felt small too. He replied by telling the Lord, "My family is poor in Manasseh, and I am the least in my father's house" (Judges 6:15). If we paraphrase his response, we see that he was in essence asking, "Lord, are You sure You are at the right address?"

It will certainly be no different for us. What has been placed in us will always be bigger than we are. We have to live up to the task and not it to us. Sometimes it is simply the enormity of the task that has been placed in our heart that baffles our mind and leaves us disillusioned. But God is no man, and He never chooses according to our strengths. Instead, He chooses according to His strength. I believe that we normally feel overwhelmed and disillusioned when we go into the triangular thinking of our own shortcomings versus the magnitude of the task versus the size of the battle. The "Who am I?" question never seems to escape us. As we are chosen by grace and not by ourselves, so is the task at hand and the battle accompanying it. The fact that we have been chosen for whatever purpose should be clue enough that we are up for both the task and the battle. We have a surety that

God will never pitch us in a battle that is out of our league. Inasmuch as He hand-picks us for certain assignments, He hand-picks our battles. The fight to bring to fulfilment our choosing may be ours, but the battle remains the Lord's.

5. Deafening-silence phase

Objective of this phase: To preserve us so that we may be effective

Most of the time after enduring the commotion and drama of being developed and having to fight our battles, we enter a phase of silence. This is a very difficult phase in the process, as our spiritual senses, once normally battle-inclined and on a high, dim when all of a sudden the battle stops. We then feel fragmented and unsure of where God is in the process. The feeling is that God has brought us thus far just to leave us. We feel forgotten by God (and people). And as much as we know from a faith perspective that what we feel is illogical, these feelings remain difficult to discard from an experiential point of view. Silence can be a powerful noise. Many a psalmist cried out to God for the deafening silence to end.

> Psalm 28:1: "Unto You will I cry, O Lord my rock; be not silent to me:"

> Psalm 83:1: "Keep not your silence, O God: hold not your peace, and be not still, O God."

This phase begs for us to wait on the Lord. I have found waiting on the Lord to be one of the most difficult Christian disciplines.

Normally we scream for help from people when we find ourselves in the heart of this phase. We long for someone to remember us and to make mention of our talents and abilities so that we may put an end to the suspense. But almost instantly after we find these people who can make mention of our talents and abilities, they forget about us. Are they bad? Not necessarily. It just means that the human hand cannot cover the full distance the hand of God wants to take us.

In Joseph's very long walk, we see this phase at work when he was in prison. Scripture reads,

> "But think on me when it shall be well with you, and show kindness, I pray you, unto me, and make mention of me unto Pharaoh, and bring me out of this house" (Genesis 40:14).

> "Yet the chief butler did not remember Joseph, but forgot him" (Genesis 40:23).

It is clear from these passages that Joseph could not take the suspense any longer, so he pleaded with the butler to make mention of him to Pharaoh. Tired of the waiting, which he perceived to be senseless, Joseph was on the brink of devising his own way out of prison. But Joseph was not in Pharaoh's prison; rather, he was a prisoner of God. The chief butler forgot about Joseph for two full years. God had put Joseph in prison, and only God had the keys to release him.

But what is the sense of all this silence?

Allow me to explain via an analogy what I believe to be the purpose of waiting on God. Earlier I referred to a very dark time my family and I had faced. After that time, our lives became uncomfortably quiet. The silence was deafening. It was inexplicable until I stumbled upon a story in a paper, a story about divers who tried to recover the body of a boy who had drowned in a certain river. The body was believed to be at a depth of more than two hundred metres. It is said that after having been submerged at such a depth for an extended period of time, a diver cannot just come up out of the water, as he could die of decompression sickness (i.e. the bends). Apparently the diver has to remain in the water for some time in order to avoid the sickness, which can be life-threatening.

This analogy, in my view, explains perfectly why we have to wait upon the Lord and why there has to be a silence after we have been through much. Sometimes we have to dive deep (i.e. emotionally, spiritually, financially and or psychologically) to lay hold of the purpose or assignment, we believe, we have been chosen for. And after we have dealt with what we were charged to do, we sometimes cannot understand why we are still circling around in the waters of our circumstances. God's main objective, I believe, for our apparent circling around when everything appears silent is to preserve us so that we may be effective in the next phase. God does not risk bringing us up too quickly, because then we could lose ourselves due to exhaustion. The Lord fully understands that we need emotional, spiritual, and psychological revitalisation after the storm, the battle, or the development or completion of an enormous task. In short, land that has not had rest cannot produce optimally.

6. Destination phase

Objective of this phase: To serve one's generation

The concept of destiny has been richly discussed in ministry, especially in Pentecostal and charismatic circles. Sometimes one gets the idea that a lot of people associate the idea of destiny with being rich or famous. In fact, the whole idea of coming into one's destiny is embedded in the idea of serving. David, the psalmist, talks about having served his generation. That, I suggest, is the gist of this phase: worshipping God and serving one's generation. Every person who has ever done anything significant has done so through serving his or her generation. King Jesus was very rich on the theme of serving. If a person wants to be great, then he or she must be willing to serve, He taught. He said that He did not come to be served, but to serve.

All of the previous phases that we have discussed are aimed squarely at getting us to our destiny. The fulfilment from this platform comes from our giving to our generation what we have received. It is this equilibrium between having received something and then giving it away that produces in us the sense of completion. Our Creator is primarily a giver. He gave Himself through the act of creation, He gave us life, and He gave us His Son. At heart, seeing that we have been created in His image and likeness, we want to be givers. We want to make meaningful contributions. But this can only happen if we give from what we have received. We normally become drained and selfish when there is a mismatch between what we want to give and what has been given to us. Such a discrepancy means that we are not true to ourselves and thus cannot truly serve our generation. What we do will not resonate back to us if such a mismatch exists. John the Baptist verbalised the idea as follows:

> "A man can receive nothing except it be given him from heaven" (John 2:27).

We can only work with what heaven has given us. When we walk into our destiny, we come to a place where we do what only we can do in relation to our sphere of influence on our generation. Our destiny is not a place we occupy in our community or workplace (it may manifest in such a way), but it is rather a place we occupy in the strategy of the kingdom of heaven. It is our platform of great influence that comes with delicate responsibility and accountability to God. It is the place where we live out our choosing and perform our purpose.

Summary of Chapter 6

1. There are six phases to the cycle of our choosing and purpose:

   - Discovery phase
   - Decision phase
   - Developmental phase
   - Disillusionment phase
   - Deafening-silence phase
   - Destination phase

2. When we reject God's choice for our lives, we are not rejecting God, but we are in essence rejecting ourselves.

3. I can't have the ability to become but not be given the free will to choose just as I can't have the free will to choose but not be given the ability to become.

4. I believe that some of our struggles start when we want to create something for ourselves outside of what has been created in us.

5. When we are in the developmental process, little of what we go through makes sense to us, which elicits contradiction in us.

6. The battle is the Lord's, but the fight is still ours.

7. The human hand cannot cover the full distance the hand of God wants to take us.

8. When we walk into our destiny, we come into a place where we do what only we can do in relation to our sphere of influence on our generation.

CHAPTER 7

IF I AM FAVOURED WHY DON'T I PROSPER?

> For behold, henceforth all generations will call me blessed.
>
> Luke 1:48

> Choosing the right path begins with submission, not information. Not even direction. Submission. Specifically, submission to the One who knows where each path leads.
>
> Andy Stanley

The choir of celestial voices still resounds because the baby Jesus has been delivered to earth. Mary and Joseph had never before witnessed anything like that which they have just witnessed. The road they have travelled since the first visitation of the angel almost a year ago feels like the lapse of one day now that they embrace their baby. Their frustration at not being able to get a place in the inn appears negligible when compared to the blissful joy stemming from their enormous sense of having accomplished their mission, the birth of the Saviour of the world. Divine peace has filled the air. The Son of God, in the body of a baby, has successfully been transferred to earth. The initiation phase of the invasion has been completed. The angelic hosts who were present witnessed the cry of the baby, a cry that registered in heaven as the child's successful landing on earth. Never before have Mary and Joseph felt such wholeness. They feel a sense of completeness born not from things or material accomplishments but from their mere obedience. The ordinary couple can still hardly believe they have been chosen for such a great purpose. They reminisce about how their lives have been impacted since they agreed to the call of God. That God, in the fragility of a child, will be in their house and under their roof every single day is a thought too vast for them to comprehend and become accustomed to. They talk about having their baby circumcised within eight days, and presented in the temple within thirty-two days, as per Mosaic law. The choice of a name has been settled by heaven. He shall be called Jesus.

Days have passed quickly. It is almost time for Mary and Joseph to prepare themselves to present their baby in the temple. The law prescribes a lamb as a sacrifice, but if a family is unable to afford a lamb, then they may bring two pigeons. An offering of two pigeons indicates that the family is poor according to the prescriptions of the law. Mary and Joseph walk into the temple and are greeted by an elderly couple, Simeon and Anna. These two people are a breath of fresh air compared to the people of the religious sects of the day. They are not misled by the ordinary appearance of Mary and Joseph, or by the two pigeons – denoting poverty – presented by them. Simeon and Anna seem to have lived for this moment, to meet the Creator in the humble form of flesh and blood. They look beyond the natural, seeing a highly favoured family with the Saviour of the world born to them, for the world. Mary and Joseph are absolutely amazed and astounded at the revelatory knowledge that Simeon and Anna possess.

The necessary ritual performed, Mary and Joseph now walk away from the temple with a renewed sense of assurance, as they have fulfilled the demands of the custom. Their conversation on the way home becomes entangled with the meaning of their being highly favoured, as they still grapple with some controversies. They can't help but think of themselves as a highly favoured poor family. "Shouldn't our being favoured have meant that we got the best place at the inn? Shouldn't being highly favoured have meant being prosperous, i.e. only having and receiving the best?" they wonder. Ending up in a manger for the grand occasion of the birth of their son, the Lord, did not quite fit with their definition of being highly favoured. Very little in their immediate visible circumstances had changed since they were apprised of their having been chosen for such a great purpose. They have their conversation about these matters not in angst. No, they are more proud than perplexed, more assured than confused Instead, the facts surrounding Christ's conception and birth, though, have not escaped their notice.

As they approach the house, Joseph suddenly starts feeling uneasy. In his heart, he feels a sense of danger gripping him. The sensation leaves him cold and anxious, but he remains uncertain as to where the sense of danger is coming from. He suppresses the emotion as he and Mary enter their home. To their surprise, wise men from the East had come to look for their baby, the Saviour. These men, like Anna and

Simeon, were not shaken by the family's humble position. They were men of faith who had travelled for months to find and worship the baby. They brought expensive gifts of gold, frankincense, and myrrh. The Magi also related to Mary and Joseph the dream they had about not returning by way of the same road.

By now, through the prophetic grapevine, the news has spread as far as Herod, the aged monarch, that the King of the Jews had been born somewhere in the land. Word has reached Mary and Joseph about Herod's discovery. Joseph now understands the sense of danger he has been having lately. He is sharply reminded about the dream he had urging him to flee with Mary and the baby into Egypt. Looking at the gifts brought by the wise men, Joseph and Mary think they now understand their purpose – to finance their journey into Egypt. They also reason that they may know something more about being prosperous and highly favoured. They conclude that prosperity produced by being chosen is tied to a cause, is inclusive of but beyond the material things of the world, and is about worshipping and knowing the plans of God.

* * *

Being chosen for a particular purpose coincides with being favoured for such a purpose. We cannot be chosen but then not be favoured to fulfil such a choice. Being favoured makes the execution of being chosen possible. A terrible tenet develops when a disconnect between being chosen and being favoured sets in. In the lives of characters such as Saul and Sampson, we witness the effect of such disconnect. The subject of being chosen will inevitably bring us to that of being favoured, which in turn will lead us to ask questions about prosperity. Our psychological theology will always draw a correlation between prosperity and being favoured; being favoured has to mean being prosperous. And there is really nothing wrong with this line of thinking, as there is more than enough biblical proof for such a position. The challenging questions arise when we see no parallel between the said favour upon our lives and our outward reality. How favoured am I when I can't even make ends meet? How favoured am I when perceivably everything goes wrong in my life? How favoured am I when nothing of what I want to do works out and I feel rather cursed?

My wife and I, at one stage of our life, had every imaginable battle on our hands. We lost our house, our car, and our furniture, and we had no resources or form of income to fall back on. We were faced with just about the most difficult set of circumstances and a seemingly impossible battle to win. This state of affairs continued not for one or two months, but for years. I had been in the Lord for more than ten years at that time, but I sensed that most unbelievers seemed to be more favoured and prosperous than I. I had found myself in such a perplexed position concerning being favoured, being chosen, and not (perceivably) being prosperous. I was forced to ask some serious questions about the concept of prosperity. My perception of prosperity had been informed by what I had heard from people, from the pulpit, and so forth, which did not match my material reality at all. It was time for me to unearth the truth about prosperity personally.

I believe that prosperity is quite a complex subject to discuss, for two reasons: firstly because it is so highly perception-driven, and secondly because there are various facets and dimensions to a person's life. Those various facets, of spirituality, emotionality, and materialism, could lead one to define prosperity according to the facet that best fits the bill, which could render a one-dimensional definition. I suggest that in its simplest form, prosperity means fruitfulness, and it is from our fruitfulness that we derive our sense of success. No person does not want to be successful.

An important characteristic of success is that it cannot be faked, at least not to oneself. We may fake it to other people, but never to ourselves. And the reason why we cannot fake it to ourselves is that there is an inward and an outward part to success. In the same way that what happens above the ground must match what happens beneath the ground in order to bring a seed to fruition, fruitfulness is always produced in a two-dimensional environment. It is never one-dimensional. Hence the phenomenon where a person can acquire a lot of material possessions and still be dissatisfied, or acquire little or no material possessions and still be satisfied. Even further, a person may acquire a lot of material possessions and be happy. In the end, whether or not we are fruitful comes down to whether or not the inward and the outward dimensions of our lives match up to produce fruitfulness.

> Genesis 2:28 reads, "And God blessed them, and said unto them, 'Be fruitful.'"

We can paraphrase that in this way: God said that humankind must be prosperous and successful.

I propose that we have to explore four broad ideas pertaining to prosperity in order to gain a better understanding of the concept. Furthermore, I suggest six vital principles within those four broad ideas that should assist us in forming a more balanced understanding of what true prosperity means.

1. Our idea of prosperity

Our *idea* of prosperity is probably the one thing, more than anything else, that can prevent us from experiencing true prosperity. In part, this is because we are sometimes more concerned about the body or the form of prosperity than we are about the essence of true prosperity. There are generally three broad perception flaws we make when forming our idea of prosperity. The first is what I refer to as the incident theory. This view dictates that a specific thing has to materialise before we are able to view ourselves as prosperous and favoured. That specific thing might vary depending on what we have set our sight on to define prosperity for us. The absence of such a thing would make it difficult for us to see ourselves as prosperous and favoured. Asaph, the writer of Psalm 73, described himself as having stumbled after he looked over a bunch of seemingly prosperous people who had everything he equated prosperity with. But after he went into the presence of God, he found that the seemingly prosperous people were not prosperous at all. This must be an indication to us that our idea of prosperity and God's view of prosperity are not necessarily the same. When we equate prosperity to a single "big" event, we discard the first principle of prosperity: prosperity is never without a course.

The second flaw to which our definition of prosperity is prone is what I refer to as the end-result perspective. When we have this perspective, we try to duplicate, usually an outward material part, in our life what we see in someone else's life without necessarily wanting to go through the processes to achieve such a result. The life of Joseph is a fitting example of this idea. The end result of everything he went through was his becoming the prince of Egypt. His brothers, for argument's sake, could not try to duplicate the end result of his life in their own lives without undergoing themselves the process he had been through. Reproducing nothing but the end result would bring about only superficial prosperity, because there would be a disconnect between the inward and outward dimension of prosperity. When we discard the inward process, we lose the substance. What we produce outwardly has its purpose embedded inwardly. The truth about why we sometimes want to duplicate just the end result is that we feel pressure to show signs of having a prosperous life. In attempting to duplicate the end result of someone else's life without going through the necessary processes ourselves, we show ourselves to be ignorant of the second principle of prosperity: prosperity is never isolated from purpose.

The third defect in our idea of prosperity is that we consider hardship to be the opposite of prosperity. Hardship and trials are not the opposite of prosperity; instead, they are (in most cases) the seed form of prosperity. They are the face of prosperity that not many can identify. Hardship is the garment prosperity sometimes wears that is not familiar to many. Hardship is an appearance we are not always keen on embracing. However, if we do not embrace the seed form of prosperity, then we will never be able to handle the end result thereof. In fact, the blessing of being fruitful by implication means that one is blessed with seed, which is a fundamental requirement to becoming fruitful. I believe the key here is not just the suffering. Mere suffering does not make us prosperous. If all we do is suffer, then we are merely great sufferers. Rather, being prosperous is about what – and how – we harvest during times of hardship and trial. It can be liken to the instructions that God gave to Moses to convey to the Israelites when they had been oppressed for almost four hundred years. Scripture tells it like this: "spoil the Egyptians" (Exodus 3:22), meaning, take hold of the gold and silver. The same silver and gold worn by the Israelites' oppressors was used to build a tabernacle in the desert. The Israelites had to take the silver and gold off their oppressors, the Egyptians. The message here is this: the seed of prosperity is often embedded in the hardship. The challenge is to shift our focus away from the actual circumstance and to start looking at the potential presented within it.

The apostle Paul at one stage wrote about taking pleasure in infirmities, in reproaches, in necessities, in persecution, and in distresses (2 Corinthians 12:10). How can anyone take pleasure in all these apparently hurtful, negative, and non-prolific propositions? What a paradox. But Paul became schooled at knowing how to draw the strength and the revelation of Christ from those things. It is from this premise that we understand that our circumstances do not denote our prosperity.

Scripture reveals this truth in reference to Joseph's life. When Joseph was in Potiphar's house, he had access to every material blessing. Scripture tells us that he was a prosperous man then (Genesis 39:2). But then Joseph ended up in prison through the lies of his master's wife. During this time, he had nothing, no access to any material blessing. He had only his life, yet scripture refers to him again as being prosperous

(Genesis 39:20–23). Here we see two completely contrasting situations in which Joseph had found himself, and in both he is referred to as prosperous.

We are not favoured because we are prosperous; rather, we are prosperous because we are favoured. If we dislike hardship, then we might just lose sight of the third principle of prosperity: prosperity is not denoted by our circumstances, but rather by the influence we have on the outcome of our circumstances.

2. Not all problems need solutions

I previously referred to a difficult time my wife and I were faced with. Prior to that time, I had almost gotten used to praying to God and then seeing God solve my problems. But for some inexplicable reason, God stopped solving my problems as I had become accustomed to. I had no understanding of what was happening. I wanted solutions, through prayer, to what I had perceived to be problems. Something had changed, irrespective of the correct prayer principles I applied. I was grappling for the known (problem equals solution) because as humans we prefer to function in the known. The space outside what is known to us is very unsettling territory. The minute we move into such territory, we naturally start looking for solutions to take us back to what feels known to us. I suggest, though, that it is imperative that we discern and distinguish between problems and paths in all our circumstances. Not everything we perceive as a problem is indeed one. If what you are facing is a problem, then there will be a solution. On the other hand, if what you are facing is part of a road you must travel to reach a more prosperous position, then there is no solution to it. It is a path that has to be travelled. And it is during such times that we sometimes tire ourselves by trying to find solutions to a path.

On Joseph's path to become ruler of Egypt we see seven key events (below) to which there was no solution. These events, however, were an indispensable part of the path:

- He was rejected by his brothers.
- He was thrown into a pit and left for dead.
- He was sold to the Midianites.
- He was sold to Potiphar.
- He was falsely accused by Potiphar's wife.
- He was imprisoned.
- The chief butler forgot him and failed to mention him to Pharaoh.

In hindsight, it is quite evident that none of these events were problems. None of them could have been "prayed away", and none of them needed a solution, because they were not problems. All of them were necessary and were an indispensable part of a greater sum: Joseph's becoming the ruler of Egypt. From this, we learn that not everything we are faced with needs to be solved. Sometimes we are linked to a path leading to a higher and more prosperous end, and some of the more painful events along the way need or have no solution. Losing sight of this fact will cause us to negate the fourth principle of prosperity: prosperity is never without a path.

3. The basis of prosperity

I suggested earlier that prosperity means, in a nutshell, being fruitful, from which we derive our sense of success, and that there are two parts to success: an inward and an outward dimension. Grasping the basis of prosperity is of utmost importance because it is from there that success stems. We referenced the scripture wherein God "blessed [humankind], and said unto them, 'Be fruitful.' From this premise has our prosperity been established. To be fruitful means to produce successfully. But of note is that the concept of fruitfulness implies that an inward seed will be manifested outwardly. Every visible living thing on the planet came about as a result of some form of inward seed. Unless the inward seed takes on an outward form, it does not constitute fruitfulness. Being prosperous thus marks our ability to produce outwardly what has been placed in us. Hence, prosperity cannot be faked, at least not to oneself. Third John 1:2 conveys the concept as follows: "Beloved, I wish above all things that you may prosper and be in health, even as your soul prospers." Paul's wish was that prosperity in other areas (outward) would follow the result of prosperity in the soul (inward). Hence it can be said that true prosperity is a reconciliation, the delivery of what is produced outwardly to that which is embedded inwardly. To define true prosperity *only* in terms of material things would be too narrow and deceptive. Seeing that prosperity can be perceived in such highly deceptive ways, it becomes highly possible to pursue prosperity as an object without necessarily pursuing the favour of God. It is thus inappropriate to pursue prosperity as an object, as true prosperity is a result. True prosperity has as its fundamental base the alignment of the inner person to the Lord, from whom the inner person receives seed inwardly to produce something outwardly.

Seeing that prosperity can be perceived in such highly deceptive ways, it becomes highly possible to pursue prosperity as an object without necessarily pursuing the favour of God.

Why is alignment to the Lord important as a base? Allow me to remind you that prosperity has to do with our ability to produce. Temptation or failure, for argument's sake, is dependent on the same principle(s) of prosperity: matching the inward seed to an outward manifestation in our lives. So when temptation or failure is successfully produced in us, we can thus say that such temptation or failure has been prosperous. The proof is the successful production process. As we always produce, we sometimes produce things, e.g. decisions, businesses, money, concepts, etc., that we cannot live and cope with in the end, because these things do not perfectly represent the initial internal concept or idea. Hence at the centre of true prosperity is the alignment and reconciliation of the inner person to the Lord. Jesus said it as follows: "I am the vine, you are the branches: He that abides in me, and I in him, the same bring forth much fruit: for without me you can do nothing" (John 15:5). "He that abides in me, and I in him" speaks to the inward part of the equation, and "the same bring forth much fruit" talks about the production and manifestation processes. The issue of prosperity is not one of whether we want to be prosperous or not. Rather, the issue of prosperity is that we have been created to be prosperous – i.e. we have the ability to produce outwardly what has been placed inwardly, whether positively or negatively. The question is not whether we are prosperous or not. We are prosperous. We were created that way. Every single person on the planet is prosperous, from the kings to the paupers. The issue is the direction of prosperity, positive or negative. The Lord created us to prosper, so the principles of prosperity are always active in our lives, whether positive or negative. It is the way we function. Our concern is not the weapon being formed against us. Weapons will always be formed. The issue is whether or not the weapon will be prosperous. Hence we are referring to the inner person's being aligned to the Lord as key. From that base, positive or true prosperity, as God intended it in creation, will emanate.

Anything we actively pursue in this world is a
reflection of our perception of glory and honour.

Thus we have the phenomenon wherein we start off with, or find ourselves in, bad circumstances, but the end turns out glorious – because the functioning of the direction of prosperity is positive. On the other hand, we see people in favourable positions ending poorly because the direction of prosperity is negative. So although we have been created to be prosperous, the alignment of the inner person to the Creator remains key in determining the direction prosperity takes. From this we derive the fifth principle of prosperity: prosperity's direction is determined by the alignment of the inner person.

4. Our inclination to honour and glory

As human beings, we appear to be inclined towards power and glory. I suggest that this has its basis in the way we have been created. When David marvelled over the creation of humankind, he uttered the following words: "For You have made him a little lower than the angels, and has crowned him with glory and honour" (Psalm 8:5).

There is no human being who naturally and readily prepares for failure and defeat. This just does not fit with human nature. All people have a genuine desire to be fruitful and successful. We were made and formed that way. It is not really the pursuit of success that makes us tick, but rather the pursuit of glory and honour. When we purely focus on the outside, the material world, for our definition of prosperity, we easily fall for deceitful or twisted derivatives of prosperity. God created us to be fruitful, to produce. Coupled with that, God made us to have a sense of glory and honour. We want glory and honour. It is what we always pursue.

Anything we actively pursue in this world is a reflection of our perception of glory and honour. It is not really the money or the careers of others that we want, but rather the access to what those things represent. We are instinctively inclined to desire anything that represents glory and honour. None of us is ever comfortable without our crown, since we were created that way, as kings and queens of the Most

High. But it is sometimes in the pure pursuit of prosperity that we chase after twisted inventions of the crown of glory and honour. When we do pursue alignment with the Lord, though, the crown of glory and honour tends to fit naturally. True glory, as per Exodus 33:18 and Exodus 34:6–7, comes as a result of the name of the Lord being bestowed upon us. When the name of the Lord is bestowed on us, it means we are His, we are chosen, and we are favoured. This is the key element that sets into motion the correct direction of the functioning of prosperity. The core elements of true glory, according to the Exodus verses named above, are as follows:

- Mercy: Experiencing God's mercy through unmerited favours
- Grace: Experiencing His strength, which enables us to accomplish things greater than our own abilities
- Long-suffering: Experiencing His patience in light of our shortcomings
- Abundant in goodness: Experiencing His abundance in health, wealth, and success
- Truth: Experiencing the truth about Him and ourselves
- Forgiveness: Experiencing His tender love
- The hand of the Lord: Experiencing His genuine involvement in our lives

In my view, these seven components of glory constitute everything any human being could ever wish for. True prosperity comes through God's crowning us with glory and honour. It is never accompanied with any pretence regarding what we have or what we've accomplished. It is the humble pursuit of God, knowing that true prosperity is our creation privilege. When we neglect pursuing the Lord, false derivatives of glory and honour will befall us, derivatives that normally result in our sorrow and brokenness. In losing sight of what true glory and honour are, we neglect the sixth principle of prosperity: prosperity is the pursuit of true glory and honour.

"For behold, henceforth all generations will call me blessed" (Luke 1:48).

Summary of Chapter 7

1. Our idea of prosperity is probably the one thing more than anything else that can prevent us from experiencing true prosperity.

2. Hardship and trials are not the opposite of prosperity but they are the seed form of prosperity.

3. It is highly possible to pursue prosperity without pursuing the favour of God.

4. Circumstances do not denote prosperity.

5. We are not favoured because we are prosperous but we are prosperous because we are favoured.

6. Everything we desire or pursue in the world is a reflection of our perception of glory and honour/power.

7. It is imperative though that we discern in all our circumstances between problems and a road. All problems have solutions but to a road there is no solution, it just has to be travelled.

8. True prosperity is God crowning you with glory and honour/power through a worshipping relationship with Him.

9. The issue of prosperity is not one of whether we want to be prosperous or not, but rather that we have been created to be prosperous- the ability to produce

outwardly what has been placed inwardly, whether positively or negatively.

10. Prosperity is never isolated from purpose.

11. It is our pursuit of God that corrects the direction of the functioning of prosperity in our lives.

CHAPTER 8

IF I AM FAVOURED, WHY DO I FACE DIFFICULT SITUATIONS MORE OFTEN THAN NOT?

He has put down the mighty from their thrones
and exalted the lowly.

Luke 1:52

God plus the world is less than God alone.
Professor William A. Dembski

The bloodthirsty despot Herod is seeking to eliminate the biggest threat, a baby, to his throne. Herod's men are canvassing the country in search of this baby. The entire country is paralysed with fear. Mary and Joseph had always been just ordinary people. But since divine favour entered their lives, they have seen a divine disruption of, and an abrupt end to, the monotony they were once caught in. As ordinary citizens of the small town of Nazareth, they have had an extraordinary roller-coaster ride of late. They have had to adapt quickly to their "new" life. Ordinariness and monotony have been quickly erased from both their vocabulary and their life. As ordinary citizens of Nazareth, they would never have dreamt that they would become the people whom Herod sought after most. The tyrant is drooling with anger and hatred. The Magi, who deceived Herod about the whereabouts of the child, have fuelled his rage to an uncontrollable level. Herod is baffled by his men's inability to find the child. What the bully doesn't understand is that the child is led by divine instruction, which Mary and Joseph execute down to the finest detail. The dictator finds himself between hysterical rage and silent insecurity, both of these things eating at him like a rodent. The celestial aura around the child renders Herod's men incompetent at tracing Him. In a moment of absolute insanity, Herod orders a broad-brush approach: the butchery of all male children younger than two years. His fear of a baby is turning him into a spectacle. The presence of a baby is causing his throne to vacillate.

On a regular basis, Mary and Joseph learn of mothers who have lost their babies and toddlers. Mary can only imagine the excruciating pain in the hearts of those mothers who had to hear their babies squealing in pain and anguish as they were slaughtered alive. How those mothers must be crying at night, clinging to their pillows whilst short of breath, as their emotional pendulum swings between longing to hold their little ones and the pain of having lost them. Those who are privileged to still have their babies live in constant fear of losing them. They clutch their babies whenever they hear the galloping of Herod's men's horses. Every time there is a knock on the door, their heart skips a beat and the blood rushes through their veins, causing them to perspire as they expect the inevitable. The whole country, almost the whole world, is gripped in a state of unimaginable pain. Mary's heart is about to faint as the enemy of her soul takes her on continuous guilt trips. "You are responsible for all the pain and grief. If you had not kept your son's identity secret, then all the pain and tears would have been prevented, because it is Him whom Herod wants. All the children who died, died because of you, Mary. You are selfish, very selfish, Mary," the enemy whispers. To all the pain the other mothers are suffering "because of her child", Mary doesn't have an answer. But looking into her baby's eyes, she experiences an indescribable hope, a hope she has never encountered before. His eyes speak to her and convey a surety that things will somehow work out. She knows there is a bigger picture, although it is not entirely clear to her, and she understands that the safekeeping of her baby is non-negotiable.

Having been on the run for months now, Mary and Joseph feel emotionally exhausted. The evil one has been very close to them at numerous times, but their awareness that heaven is counting on them has kept them going. As the days unfolded, an immovable trust in divine providence broke through in their hearts. They have outgrown many of their fears, as they have come to discover that they are not as small as they once thought they were. As conventional people, with a gift placed in their care, they have outmanoeuvred the fiercest despot on the face of the earth. They feel a sense of elevation and growth in their hearts as they keep on clinging to heaven's gift.

* * *

When purpose is in its infancy, we have a responsibility to protect it from a premature death. We ought to give ourselves wholeheartedly to the survival of what we have been purposed to do when it is in the earliest stage. It is heaven's gift to us. Sometimes keeping it alive entails fleeing from certain circumstances, business deals, relationships, etc. If we live in a prepared manner to sustain our potential, then our purpose, now in its infancy, will later sustain us. I think it is interesting that we rarely (and I am not saying that this is a rule) turn out to do on the "big stage" anything other than what we have been doing on a small scale. In fact, in most cases, the very thing we failed at in the beginning is the thing we get called to do later. Simply because we failed at it the first time makes us likely not to want to make any future attempts at doing the same thing. It is almost like moving into the proximity of a certain radius from where we get a slight signal of what we should do, then going on to do exactly that, and then failing at it.

From the story of Moses, it is evident that in his heart he believed he would have something to do with the deliverance of Israel. He killed one Egyptian and was driven out of Egypt, only to get called back to perform the same mission again. The disciples were fishermen all their lives. Most importantly, they were fishermen at heart. Instead of Jesus's calling them away from the art of fishing, He placed a kingdom directive on what they had been doing all their lives by ordaining them to become fishers of men. David must have been one of the best shepherds of his day. When God anointed him, He did not call him away from shepherding as such, but rather He placed a kingdom directive on him to shepherd His people. I believe that when we pick up the "signal" of our choosing, we sometimes move out prematurely in wanting to perform what we have been chosen to do. When we move ahead too quickly, though, we almost always fail at our first attempt. To God, though, I believe that it is not a train smash. I suggest that to God it is more important that we come into contact with the signal of our choosing than that we fail at the attempt. The failure will be ironed out as we grow in the stature of our purpose and choosing.

The growth-process is, at times, mercilessly tough on us, yet it is so irreplaceably essential that we would eventually sink without it.

One of my favourite pictures of Junior, my son, is one wherein he is two years old and wearing his grandfather's boots. Just his being in his nappy with the boots covering him up to his knees was very cute to witness. And the cuteness to this picture lies in the disproportion between Junior's size and that of the boots. Twenty years from that point, there will be no cuteness in Junior's wearing his grandfather's boots, because there will no longer be a disproportion in size. The boots will never increase in size, but Junior's feet will. I think that is the view the Father has. Once we have the hint of what we should do, we are ready to be grown in stature and understanding of our purpose. People will always find it hilarious when we do not (yet) fit the shoes of what we believe we are supposed to accomplish. They may find the disproportion laughable, but God is pleased that we have picked up the signal of our calling. From that premise, He grows us to eventually fit the shoes of our passion.

Think of the many people who accomplished great things but who started out by being dubbed as fools, as hilarious, and as cute because they started off not fitting the shoes of their passion. David's father (and brothers) found the disproportion between David's shepherding sheep and being anointed to be very funny. Because of this, David was not called to be considered for ordination as king. David's relatives never thought that there was a link between shepherding sheep and being the king of Israel. But God knew there was a link. By the same token, people of the religious orders of Jesus's day never thought there could be a link between being a fisherman and becoming an apostle of the New Testament church, but God knew there was a link.

We often stand in the right shoes, but those shoes might be just a tad too big for us. Hence the growth process beckons. Such a process is not always pleasurable, as it can sometimes stretch us to the point where we feel we cannot take any more. The growth process is, at times, mercilessly tough on us, yet it is so irreplaceably essential that we would eventually sink without it. Such a process is essentially an enlargement process, both spiritually and emotionally. And going through it sometimes gives one a sinking feeling – the feeling of walking in a desert.

[1]I recall one of my physical science questions at school about a springbok and a camel walking in the desert. The question was, "Why is it easier for a camel than for a springbok to walk in the desert?" What makes this question interesting is the fact that the camel is so much larger in size than the springbok, yet it finds it easier to walk in the sinking sands of the desert. The answer to the question lies in the size of each animal's feet. The principle is this: the bigger the surface of the foot, the less the pressure exerted on the ground. Because the camel's feet are bigger, less pressure is exerted when

the camel walks, and therefore the animal doesn't sink into the sand. The springbok's feet are smaller, and hence the springbok experiences more pressure, sinks deeper into the sand, and finds it extremely difficult to walk in the desert. The point here is this: if we don't grow, then chances are we will sink when we are confronted with the challenges of our choosing. Any enlargement process will always push and stretch our limitations, some of which have been placed on us either by other people or by our own thinking.

I suggest that there are two indispensable laws that govern the growth process. The first law is that growth has to happen proportionally. The second law is that growth has to happen naturally. If these two laws are violated or otherwise not adhered to, then death as a result of growth is inevitable. Death is the common end result when we grow too fast and when we do not grow at all.

Proportional growth

[2]I remember the story of a boy born in the Transkei a number of years back. His size caused such an uproar at the time. He grew rapidly and at a seemingly unstoppable pace. At the age of about four years, he had the weight and height of an average twelve-to fourteen-year-old. Sadly, he didn't live long. He suffered a premature death because his growth was both unnatural for, and disproportionate to, his age. In the business world, it is no different. In early 2000, an investment company started an investment fund. In late 2003 and early 2004, that company announced its concern about the rapid growth of the fund, as rapid growth is also a sign of premature collapse due to the lack of sustainability.

Any enlargement process will always
include a mixture of powerful emotive sources
such as betrayal, hurt, condemnation, deceit,
and success.

The phenomenon of disproportional growth occurs when the growth that happens in facets of our lives do not happen in us. Disproportional growth becomes prevalent when our character cannot sustain the growth in other areas (such as business, finance, society, etc.) of our lives, thereby leading to an internal collapse. Internal growth is the antidote to disproportional growth, but internal growth can only happen as a result of an enlargement process. Such a process can sometimes be very confusing because it brings a mixture of emotions. Any enlargement process will always include a mixture of powerful emotive sources such as betrayal, hurt, condemnation, deceit, and success. This process will stir in us our potential to become bitter or better, smaller or bigger. It is a process that produces motion in us, with the aim of producing sustainability.

In the previous chapter, we spoke about the fact that we have been created to produce. But to continually produce, we must continually grow. Sustainability is the aspect of growth that ensures that we have a continuous inward capacity to produce. In most cases, we build inward sustainability by going through resistant situations. These are situations that feel and look stronger than we are. We normally refer to them as difficult situations. What we experience as difficult has a lot to do with our perceived limitations and our ability to adapt. I am using the phrase "perceived limitations", as many of our limitations are either self-imposed or imposed upon us by others. Being placed in difficult circumstances gives us the opportunity to test and examine the reality of such limitations.

[3]It is said that breaking the cocoon of a butterfly in its pupa stage is the worst favour one could do for the insect. Apparently the butterfly's wings have to break open the cocoon; otherwise, the butterfly will have a shortened lifespan. Keeping this in mind, we sometimes feel that other people are far away from us when we (feel) that we are facing our most difficult situations. The reality is that people are sometimes not supposed to be there to help break open our "cocoon". Our breaking through our own limitations is God's way of allowing us to build long-term sustainability inside us. We have to reinforce the point that we don't grow simply because we are faced with difficult situations. Unless we grow our capacity for sustainability in those circumstances, we do not grow at all.

To create a capacity for sustainability, one must be willing and able to take one's available resources, be it energy, insight, finance or strategy, and then merge and harmonise them with the (difficult) circumstances. It is highly possible to find oneself in difficult circumstances without any form of growth taking place. One can be in such situations and merely become used to them without ever growing. Unless we merge and harmonise what we have and apply it to the situation, we do not grow. Merging and harmonising experiences is exactly what David did to outgrow being a shepherd of sheep. He entered a situation for which Saul and his men had no answer: a battle against Goliath. Saul gave David his armour to employ in the situation, but it was too heavy, not sustainable. Instead of using Saul's armour, David decided to merge and harmonise what he had (his slingshot and the mental picture of his having destroyed the bear and the lion), and to apply those things to the situation. This caused him to outgrow his position as shepherd, which set him on a sustainable path to the palace.

Natural growth

Growth will always produce influence and the sphere of our influence will always increase as we grow. We can refer to our sphere of influence as our territory, which we can define as an area within our control or under our ownership. The one who has control or ownership has a right and authority over that area that no other person has. All of us have a territory, a sphere of influence. Scripture teaches us that God "has determined [the nations'] pre-appointed times and the boundaries of their dwellings" (Acts 17:26). Each and every one of us has been placed divinely within a specific territory.

The functioning of favour over our lives is a key determinant that impacts the sphere of our influence. When Joseph was put in prison after Potiphar's wife lied about him, the sphere of his influence was reduced to a mere prison cell. But the functioning of God's favour upon his life enlarged his territory from being in a prison cell to governing a nation. I believe that this was so because the growth in Joseph was systematic, which is the antidote to unnatural growth.

Numerous times in scripture, the human body is referred to as the temple of God, His dwelling place. If we are said to be the tabernacle of God, then I suggest that the territory of our lives takes after the pattern of the tabernacle in the Old Testament.

The tabernacle had three areas:

- The outer court
- The inner court
- The holy of holies

Unsystematic growth means that we grow from
the outside in.

All three of these areas were part of the tabernacle, with the
only difference between each being the level of intimacy. The
territory of our lives can, by comparison to the tabernacle,
be illustrated as follows:

Outer Court	Inner Court	Holy of Holies
(Least intimate part of our lives)	(More intimate part of our lives)	(Most intimate part of our lives)
Representing the functional aspect of our lives (work/career)	Representing the relational aspect of our lives (family/friends)	Representing the personal aspect of our lives (the true self)

Our personal lives represent the most intimate part of our
lives – our identity, our essence. The inner court speaks to
the relational aspect of our lives – our family and friendships.

The outer court represents the functional side of our lives – what we do. When we stop growing in the most intimate part of ourselves, the holy of holies, and yet continue to grow in other parts of our lives, we set ourselves up for an internal collapse. Such growth, where we grow from the outside in, would constitute unsystematic growth, which is unnatural. The antidote to unnatural growth is natural growth, which is systematic in nature and which happens from the inside out to affect the whole sphere of our life. The depth of the foundation of our personal life determines the height of the building in the outer court of our life. When God intends to grow our territory, He normally starts *in us* and then circles out into the inner court (relational aspects) and the outer court (functional aspects) of our life.

When I travel from one town to another, the different statues on display always fascinate me. It is interesting to me that these statues are seldom, if ever, life-size reflections of the people they represent. They are almost always larger than the life-size reflections of the people they represent. To me, such statues are reminiscent of how busy we sometimes are at trying to erect statues of ourselves in the territory of our lives. And I think we like erecting these types of statues because they give us a larger reflection of ourselves. The danger starts when our stature cannot uphold our statues. When our statue becomes disproportionally larger than our stature, trouble lurks. We normally erect such statues in the inner and outer courts of our lives. But it is in the holy of holies, the deeper inner self, where stature has to be developed. The statues we erect are representative of all the legacies we try to leave behind in the inner and outer court of our lives, but they require the stature from the inner self to uphold them. Growth in stature means that we have developed in character, as our character determines our capacity to contain and distribute God's favour. When America invaded Iraq, the first thing that US soldiers toppled was a statue of Saddam Hussein. Perhaps because Hussein's stature could not uphold the statue, that statue was the first to fall. When the enemy of our soul invades our territory, it won't be our statues that will keep him out. Rather, the stature of our inner man will have to stand up to defend our territory.

It is God's design that the growth in us serve as a vehicle to transport His favour to other territories of our lives. The scriptures teach us that Jesus grew in stature and in the favour of God. The reason for such design is this: God does not want us to be successful for a season, but for a lifetime. And the only way to be successful for a lifetime is through continual growth, which produces the capacity for sustainability.

The danger starts when our stature cannot
uphold our statues.

God does not want to bless our endeavours without our having the blessing. There is no glory to God in having the inner and outer court of our territory enlarged whilst *we* remain small on the inside. We normally err in trying to take the measurement of our territory ourselves. We can never know the width and length of our lives. Should we take a measurement of our life, we only limit ourselves. God is the One with the true measuring line. When we allow Him to measure the length and width of our territory, and we permit the accompanying growth process to start within us, we will find ourselves surprised at what He wants to achieve through us.

We can illustrate the dynamics of growth as follows:

Growth Law	Violation	Antidote
1. Proportional	Disproportional	Growth in us
2. Natural	Unnatural	Systematic growth in territory

An important point to emphasise is that as we develop and grow, we do so in the heat and heart of what life throws at us. Our growth does not happen outside of the day-to-day activities of life. No. It happens in the midst of difficult situations, simultaneous and parallel to them. Ou growth occurs as on-the-job training. Therefore, our growth and the next phase of the manifestation of what has been planted inside of us happen as different sides to the same coin. The next phase is the next opportunity, the next moment which we have to seize.

"He has put down the mighty from their thrones and exalted the lowly" (Luke 1:52).

Summary of Chapter 8

1. The growth process is, at times, mercilessly tough on us, yet it is so irreplaceably essential that we would eventually sink without it.

2. There are two laws that govern growth. The first law is that growth has to happen proportionally. The second law is that growth has to happen naturally.

3. Disproportional growth happens when our character cannot sustain growth in certain areas (such as business, finance, society, etc.) of our lives, thereby leading to a premature collapse.

4. Any enlargement process will have a mixture of betrayal, hurt, condemnation, deceit, and success to it.

5. Unsystematic growth means that we grow from the outside in. Systematic growth means that we grow from the inside out.

6. When our statue becomes disproportionally larger than our stature, an internal collapse is imminent.

CHAPTER 9

THE BIRTH OF FAVOUR

> The stumbling-block for that age was not so
> much the Lord's divinity as his crucifixion,
> Because he suffered, said the Jew, he was not
> divine. Because he was divine, replied the
> Gnostic, he did not suffer.
>
> H. M. Gwatkin

It has been thirty-three years since Mary heard the declaration "You are Highly Favoured" from the angel. She undoubtedly still remembers the overwhelming excitement the appearance of the angel and his announcement brought to her. She remembers her visit to Elizabeth and how they discussed the possible outcome of their children's lives. She remembers Jesus as a baby and how He grew up in front of her. Flashes of Him staying behind in the temple at the age of twelve, telling her and Joseph that He had to do the business of His Father, go through her mind. For the past three years, she and the crowds have witnessed Jesus perform miracle after miracle. She remembers His first miracle, at the wedding in Cana, where He turned water into wine. The many deaf and blind people who received healing from

Him come to mind. He was thronged by the crowds as they witnessed supernatural power flowing from His hands. His teachings were fresh, and people sought a daily dose thereof.

But today it is different. There is a stark contrast between today and the past thirty-three years. In fact, today the words "You are Highly Favoured" appear to be hanging on a very thin thread of life amidst the shouts of, "Crucify Him. Crucify Him." It emerges that the bloodthirsty crowd will have their demands met. For Mary, the prospect of losing her son feels like a sword piercing her soul. What is about to happen is completely dissimilar to the atmosphere in which the angel appeared, the excitement all the miracles brought, and the surety of all the promises and prophecies. Yesterday started as a "normal" day, a day in which anything could happen, because a day with Jesus always proved to be unpredictable. In His presence, Mary, the disciples, and the multitudes have come to accept the miraculous as the norm, the impossible as possible, and the supernatural as natural. But since He was taken captive last night, an uncertainty has gripped Mary, the disciples, and those close to them. The day when she and Joseph went to the temple to present Him as a baby flickers through her memory. She can remember Him as a baby, totally dependent on her and Joseph's care. The words of Simeon, "A sword shall pierce His own soul," burst through her mind like a flash of lightning on a dark, stormy plain. "Is this that day?" she asks herself as her heart grows cold and her body anxious. But she is still expectant of a miracle.

Peter and the other disciples have been following the ordeal since last night. In the garden they witnessed an intensity about Him that they had never seen before. His intensity was almost a nervousness that they could neither trace nor share. Last night He pleaded with them, like one frightened, to pray an hour with Him. He woke them every now and then, but they, not experiencing the same intensity, inexorably fell asleep each time. There was a casualness about them, as the hour was concealed from them. They found themselves in a place of complete ease, which in part stemmed from the trust they had developed over the last three years. They had seen storms calmed, thousands fed with five loaves, Him walking on water, incurable diseases being healed, demons cast out, Lazarus being raised from the dead, and much more. So what could be difficult or insurmountable to Him? What could cause Him to become anxious and nervous? What could cause Him to perspire apprehensively and lead Him to pass a sleepless night?

His disciples had followed Him from the garden with a nonchalant trust, knowing that a miracle to save Him must be a mere formality away. Peter promised Him that he would die with Him, but he based his promise on his Master's immortality. "He cannot die, can He?" Peter asked himself. As the events unfold, the disciples follow, waiting for that miraculous intervention.

The further the events unfold, the further the contradiction and confusion in them grows – and the less of them remain. The prospect and likelihood that He is going to be crucified and die is taking shape and stature as the hope of the awaited miracle fades away. Confused, perplexed, and with dashed hopes, the disciples turn away one by one.

Mary's heart is on the cusp of bursting as Jesus is about to be crucified. The atmosphere is filled with an incomprehensible heaviness, something completely unfamiliar to the bystanders. Jesus is unrecognisable on the cross. His face is utterly disfigured as darkness starts covering the face of the earth. Through the darkness, Jesus is barely visible. The voice of the crowd becomes silent as inexplicable darkness covers the land. From the obscure figure on the cross emanates a thunderous voice, crying, "My God, My God, why has Thou forsaken Me?" Minutes later, Jesus dies. Mary is shocked and inconsolable. Life has died, the Resurrection will be buried, the Way has come to an end, the Beginning has reached extinction, the Door has closed, and the Light has been quenched. One of the Roman soldiers looks on in shock and awe as Jesus's blood drips from his hand and his hammer. The authoritative voice from the cross echoes through the chambers of his heart as he remembers Jesus's cry, "Father forgive them for they know not what they do". The soldier is gripped by a sense of shame and guilt as he stares at the drops of blood from his hand and his hammer falling to the ground. He is subdued in confession as he acknowledges, "Truly He was the Son of God."

But Mary and all the others are completely unaware of the prelude to the summit, before Gabriel was called to convey to her that she had been chosen and highly favoured. Before Gabriel was called, the Word agreed to become flesh, to take on the form of a man so that the demands of a holy God could be met and be reconciled with the beings that were formed in His image and likeness. For the next three days, Mary and the rest of Jesus's followers will battle with this paradox, only to understand it once this three-day period is over.

The declaration "You are highly favoured" is God's assurance to every human being who has the faith to answer

His call. This assurance comes irrespective of our failures, weaknesses, and imperfections. In fact, God doesn't expect us to be perfect. Rather, He expects us to rest in Jesus's perfection. He doesn't expect us to be "right" but rather to rest in Jesus's righteousness. We have been "fearfully and wonderfully made"[1], and are special and precious in God's eyes. He will always care about us. The favour we have spoken about in the pages of this book came at a cost to us. Also, it cost God everything. God's description of everything He created was, "It is good." However, the entrance of sin through humankind's own choice changed that unadulterated picture of everything that was created. The Word of God actually shows a different picture of God's heart towards humankind after sin had entered the world through humankind's disobedience and choice. The picture is recorded as follows:

> "And it repented the Lord that He had made man on the earth and *it grieved Him in his heart.* And the Lord said, I will *destroy man* whom I have created from the face of the earth; both man and beast and the creeping thing, and the fowls of the air; for it repents me that I have made them. But Noah *found grace* in the eyes of the Lord." (Genesis 6:6–8, emphasis added)

These few verses contain a portrait of God's heart, a heart deeply broken, darkened by humankind's sin through disobedience, and filled with rejection of human beings, you and I included. The phrase "grieved His heart" and the word "repented" convey the message that God sighed heavily in sadness because He had made humankind. One can sense the clear disconnect between God's intention for creating humankind and the reality created by humankind's sin through choice. God's intention was to create a being that would follow after His likeness, image, and nature, not one that would produce evil continually. The destruction of humankind in the days of Noah did not start with the flood. It started in God's heart. God was desperate for a new beginning, desperate to re-establish His original intent for humankind. God's one characteristic that stopped Him from completely destroying the human race was grace, also known as favour[2]. Favour stood between humankind's complete extinction and humankind's survival. In Noah, God found a temporary solution, but after the flood humankind progressively drifted down the same sinful slope again. Once again, the picture of grief and sadness was opened in God's heart. Humankind just wouldn't change. The solution to humankind's sinful heart was still grace (favour), but this time around it was a different application of grace. We had to be given access to grace to thus become partakers of grace. Acceptance of this access to grace would enable humanity to rule over the power of sin and thus permit them to walk in God's original intent for them and fulfil their given potential. The Hebrew term for grace, "Hen"[3], means, "a strong man moved by the need of a weaker and coming to his aid". But God was going to take this farther than just coming to the aid of the weaker. He wanted to complete the picture by coming to *live* in the weaker vessel. In order for this to happen, humankind had to be granted access to God's heart and God access to humanity's heart. Only a change in humankind's heart would enable human beings to pursue and follow God's original intent. Such a change of heart could only be made possible through a flow of grace from God's heart. The flow of grace had to flow from God's heart to humankind's heart because humanity was incapable to bring about the desired change. But, in order for grace to reach the heart of humankind, God's heart[4] had to be changed first. Healing and restoration, from the grief, sadness, and disappointment induced by people's choice to deviate from God's original intent for humankind, needed to be brought to God's heart. The picture of God's grief, repentance, and sadness over the creation of humankind had to be changed first. God, if you will, had to have a "heart transplant", which could only be done by His Son, Jesus Christ.

At the birth of Jesus, we see a completely different picture of God's heart being presented. Angles rejoiced in humankind, sang the praises of God and announced a new beginning for humanity in their relationship with God, ushered in by grace (favour). The words "You are Highly Favoured" to Mary ushered in the vehicle of grace (favour), i.e. the strong One would come to live in the weak. The song the angels sang in Luke 2:14, "Glory to God in the highest, and on earth peace, goodwill toward men," appears a complete contrast to the feelings of grief and sadness that God had towards humankind in Genesis 6:6–8. With the birth of Christ, we have a picture of rejoicing in, and goodwill towards, humankind. Heaven brought the message that God had declared Himself willing to undergo a "heart transplant". In His infinite wisdom, God decided that a place called Calvary would be used as the place for the "heart transplant".

> John 19:17: "And He bearing His cross went
> forth into a place called the place of a skull,
> which is called in the Hebrew Golgotha."

The cross for a crucifixion included a vertical and a horizontal beam. The vertical beam was planted at the place of crucifixion. The person to be crucified had to carry the horizontal beam to the crucifixion site. The cross of Jesus and its associated suffering and shame were going to be the instruments used to "open" the heart of God and remove the grief and repentance He had felt over the creation of humankind. God's heart, through the cross of Jesus, would be opened to blessing and expressing goodwill towards humankind.

> Mark 15:33: "And when the sixth hour was come, there was darkness over the whole land until the ninth hour."

I believe that the darkness spoken about when Jesus hung on the cross was not an eclipse. Neither was it the presence of satan. That darkness, I propose to you, was the grief, repentance, and sadness in God's heart caused by humankind's deviation from His original intent. God was in an "operating theatre". All the other sacrifices, animal blood and covenants, only served as instruments of temporary respite to what God had felt. Only Jesus's sacrifice could change God's heart towards humankind. It took a three-hour "operation" to remove the grief, sadness, and disappointment from God's heart caused by humankind's infidelity and high treason. And the fact that it didn't stay dark whilst Jesus was on the cross served as evidence that the "heart transplant" was successful.

> Mark 15:37–38: "And Jesus cried with a loud voice and gave up the ghost. And the veil of the temple was rent in twain from top to bottom."

The veil separated the holy place from the most holy place (Exodus 23:33). Not just anyone could enter into the most holy place. The high priest went into the most holy place once a year to make offerings on behalf of the people. But when Jesus gave His flesh (life) on Calvary, the veil was torn in two. Rocks were split, the earth shook, and the graves were opened when God's manifest presence left the "building". The stage was set for the strong One to come live in the weak. God has always desired to have a relationship with humankind. A visitation once a year, when the high priest entered the most holy place, was never God's ideal. God "left the building" to come and live in us so that we could become partakers of His favour. But the work of grace was only completed when Christ Jesus ascended on high. God's invitation now reads, "Let us therefore come boldly to the *throne of grace,* that we may obtain mercy and find grace to help in time of need" (Hebrews 4:11, emphasis added).

There is no clear indication of how many thrones there are in heaven. Could it be that the throne of grace was instituted only after Jesus performed the work of grace on Calvary? Could this be a "new" throne instituted by God for you and me? I choose to believe so because Jesus Christ brought us "truth and grace" (John 1:17). This throne was instituted not for the angels or the other celestial beings but for the human race. It doesn't matter what our soul sickness or weakness might be; the answer lies in the throne of favour, where we "may obtain mercy and find grace to help in time of need". God smiles over us. No longer do we have to walk as strangers to His promises. We don't have to be in this world without hope and without God, because now we can become partakers of His grace. The cross of Jesus Christ has destroyed the alienation between God and us. God's heart towards us has been changed. The King of Kings is sitting on the throne of favour and waiting for us to draw closer. His sceptre is pointing towards you and me. Access has been granted. It is this very same grace that empowers us to fulfil the purpose that God has laid in our heart. It is this grace – the fact that God takes pleasure in you and me – that covers the full distance in the race that we have to run in order to give birth to what we are chosen to do.

There is no reason, logical or illogical, that can prevent us from fulfilling what has been placed in our hearts. The price that was paid to bring favour right to our heart's doorstep was too big for us to fail at our calling. The strong One living in the weak means that irrespective of the dilemma you might face in fulfilling your choosing, you can.

CONCLUSION

For behold, henceforth all generations will call
me blessed.

Luke 1:48

Throughout the previous chapters, I have shown that
producing what God has gifted us with is not easy, but neither
is it impossible. The road to produce such potential lies
somewhere between easy and impossible. It is a road filled
with grace, without which we will never bring to fruition our
choosing and purpose. Once purpose has been birthed in
our heart, we are compelled to make certain adjustments to
give ourselves and the gift within us a chance at success. We
may be required to prioritise our actions, our time, and our
energy accordingly. As life is not lived in a straight line, it
becomes imperative that we learn how to be flexible in order
to deal with what life throws at us whilst we are in pursuit
of fulfilling our choosing. What we do may not always go
according to plan, but as long as we remain cause-driven we
will prevail. In our seen reality there may be things missing
in relation to what we have seen in our hearts. Other things
may not seem to make sense, and still other things may seem

161

impossible, as we pursue what we believe to be our purpose. But in the midst of whatever dilemma we may face as a result of our having been chosen, God's favour (grace) will be the balancing item to correct the scale.

Warmly,

M. C. Van Rensburg

ENDNOTES

Introduction

[1] I have chosen to discard the grammatical rules by not writing any reference to the enemy in capital letters. The foe has caused me too much distress.

Chapter 1: What is Favour

[1] Collins Compact Dictionary, 6th ed. Harper Collins Publishers, 2004

[2] There are disparate theological views on the link between humankind's actions and the well-being and age of the earth. Depending on the view one chooses, the issue of a young earth versus an old earth comes into play. For me it is difficult to separate humankind's actions from the well-being of the earth. It was because of Adam's disobedience that the ground was cursed. Professor William A. Dembski, in The End of Christianity, B&H Publishing Group: Nashville, Tenessee, 2009, (Chapters 5-7) makes some very interesting arguments about the age of the earth. Also, Mark Whorton and Hill Roberts, Holman QuickSource Guide to Understanding Creation, B&H Publishing Group: Nashville, Tennessee, 2008 makes for insightful reading on the subject of the age of the earth.

3   Romans 8:22. For me, this also underlines the fact that humanity's actions did (do) have a bearing on creation.

4   Genesis 1:26. This is such a fundamental verse (utterance) about the existence of humankind and about the action and reaction of God in relation to humanity's disobedience. This verse, when considering its simplest interpretation, means that God ordained humanity as His representative, which also gave God the legal right to represent humankind on the cross through the person of Jesus Christ.

5   Professor William A. Dembski, *The End of Christianity*, B&H Publishing Group: Nashville, Tennessee, 2009. In positioning the point on biasness of favour here, I heavily borrow from what Professor Dembski aptly and succinctly argues in the chapter "The Reach of the Cross" (p. 25). Professor Dembski quotes G. K. Chesterton on exercising the will: "Every act of will is an act of self-limitation. To desire action is to desire limitation. In that sense every act is an act of self-sacrifice. When you choose anything, you reject everything else." *The End of Christianity* is one those must-have books.

Chapter 2: If I Am Favoured, Why Is My World Falling Apart?

1   The late Dr Myles Munroe's book *Understanding the Purpose and Power of Prayer Earthly License for Heavenly Interference, Whitaker House: New Kensington, 2002* is an excellent resource to have on the subject of prayer.

2   The position of the uniqueness of our talents and giftings is what I refer to as our bias predicate. It is from this position that we are favoured and blessed. Every person has a bias predicate.

3   Philip Yancey, in *The Bible Jesus Read, Zondervan, Grand Rapids, Michigan, 1999, 67*: aptly refers to such behaviour as "contract faith". In a nutshell, this means a reward/punishment relationship with God. In the same part 2, "Job:

Seeing in the Dark", Philip Yancey brilliantly explains our cosmic interlinkage

Chapter 3: If I Am Favoured, Why Don't I Think So?

[1] The mind, I believe, is more than the brain. When God breathed the breath of life and the man became a "living soul" (Genesis 2:7) was the point when humankind received an independent mind with an ability to choose independently. Dr Caroline Leaf. *Who Switched Off My Brain? Toxic Thoughts, Emotions& Bodies*, The Switch On Your Brain Organisation, 2007, is a brilliant practical guide on the workings and effects of the thoughts on the brain.

[2] James Strong. The New Strong's Exhaustive Concordance of eh Bible, Thomas Nelson, Inc. Nashville, Tennessee, 1990, "Hebrew and Chaldee Dictionary", 51 (3335).

[3] Steven R. Covey, *The Seven Habits of Highly Effective People, New York: Simon & Schuster, 1989.*

Chapter 4: If I am Favoured, Why Don't I Know My Purpose

[1] Collins Compact Dictionary, 6th ed. Harper Collins Publishers, 2004

Chapter 5: If I Am Favoured, Why Are People Deserting Me

[1] Josh McDowell, The Best of Josh McDowell: A Ready Defense. Here's Life Publishers, Inc., San Bernardino, CA, 1990, 210. This is one book on apologetics that I revisit regularly.

Chapter 8: If I Am Favoured, Why Do I Face Difficult Situations More Often Than Not?

[1]   This was one of my exam questions in Grade 10 (then Standard 8), in 1989. I recall that the question appeared in most of my physical science classes that year.

[2]   I was somewhere between six and eight years old when this story made such an uproar. I remember following the story with childhood concern as my mother read to me every article about the incident.

[3]   I am not sure who to accredit this to, but I first heard Pastor Ray McCauley preach on this in one of his sermons.

Chapter 9: The Birth of Favour

[1]   Guy P. Duffield and Nathaniel M. Van Cleave, Foundations of Pentecostal Theology, p. L.I.F.E. Bible College at Los Angeles, 1983, p.119, Guy P. Duffield and Nathaniel M. Van Cleave quote Dr Paul Brand and Philip Yancey from Fearfully and Wonderfully Made (Grand Rapids, MI: Zondervan Publishing House, 1981) on some mind-boggling realities about how the human body had been "assembled". In short:
The body senses infinitesimal differences with unfailing scent; it knows its hundred trillion cells by name. ... My body is more like a fountain than a sculpture: maintaining its shape, but constantly being renewed. Somehow my body knows the new cells belong, and they are welcomed. ... DNA is estimated to contain instructions that, if written out would fill a thousand, six hundred–page books ... yet if the DNA were unwound and joined together end to end, the strand would stretch from the earth to the sun and back more than four hundred times.

[2]   James Strong. *The New Strong's Exhaustive Concordance Of The Bible*, Thomas Nelson, Inc. Nashville, Tennessee, 1990, "Hebrew and Chaldee Dictionary". ; 41 (2580).

3   Lawrence O. Richards, *Richards' Complete Bible Handbook,* Word Inc., *1982;* 716.

4   By writing that God had a "heart transplant", I am not suggesting that God harboured hatred. Instead, I am merely suggesting that the sin of humankind had an impact on God's heart. And just as creation emanated from the heart of God, so do the salvation and restoration of humankind emanate from the heart of God.